Paula Pryke's
simple flowers

Paula Pryke's simple flowers

paula pryke

photography by **james merrell**

RYLAND
PETERS
& SMALL
LONDON NEW YORK

For Coco

First published in the United States in 1999 as *Simple Flowers*
This edition published in 2006 by
Ryland Peters & Small
519 Broadway, 5th Floor
New York, NY 10012
www.rylandpeters.com

10 9 8 7 6 5 4 3 2 1

ISBN-13: 978-1-84597-240-0
ISBN-10: 1-84597-240-6

Publishing Director Anne Ryland
Senior Designer Penny Stock
Assistant Designer Sailesh Patel
Senior Editor Hilary Mandleberg
Editor Jane Struthers
Production Patricia Harrington
Stylist Martin Bourne

Printed in China

Library of Congress Cataloging-in-Publication Data

Pryke, Paula.
    [Simple flowers]
    Paula Pryke's simple flowers / Paula Pryke ; photography by James Merrell.
        p. cm.
    Rev. ed. of: Simple flowers. 1999.
    Includes index.
    ISBN-13: 978-1-84597-240-0
    1. Flower arrangement. 2. Cut flowers. 3. Flowers. I. Title: Simple flowers. II.
Pryke, Paula. Simple flowers. III. Title.
    SB449.P7923 2006
    745.92'2–dc22
                                                        2005034815

contents

introduction

Simple Flowers is my most personal book to date. It shows the way I like to arrange flowers in my own home. Although they may be placed in many different locations, each is an example of my preferred style of arrangement for a particular position. Often the interior or the vase dictates which flowers should be used, or the flowers themselves cry out for a special type of arrangement. But whichever way you begin the process, the flowers remain the stars of the show, enlivening an interior or turning a special container into a living statement.

Flowers have the ability to redefine our lives and our spirits. This book attempts to convey the exquisite beauty of flowers which, if we allow it, will invade our emotions with the purest expression of joy. In short, Simple Flowers is for people who love flowers and who cannot imagine life without them.

My work often requires me to fashion grand and lavish arrangements for friends or clients. However, when they are finished I sometimes pause for a moment to think about the natural simplicity of flowers and to wonder whether the measured admiration of a few blooms is not more rewarding than the overwhelming impact of a hugely complicated design. Often it is the simple displays that give me the greatest creative buzz.

Whenever I attend industry conventions that showcase new designs in flower creativity, I am always impressed by my colleagues' imagination and technical skill in creating new concepts. But I know that when I retreat to my own home I will always prefer to fill it with beautiful, simple flower arrangements in which I can watch the whole process of flowering from bud to full bloom. In simple groupings the flowers speak for themselves – the designer is silent.

Too much has been written recently about fashion flowers. We are told which are the most popular and which have passed from grace into disrepute. Although journalists frequently phone me to ask my opinion on which flowers are in or out of fashion, I always hate to nominate losers. To me they are all winners. Whenever I am given flowers, however modest they may be, I marvel at their very existence and revel in the generosity of the giver. Never do I think of a gift of flowers as a fashion statement. Flowers are friends you love for their character and personality, not for the way they look or dress.

my love of flowers

started as early as I can remember. As a child I used to wander around the water meadows surrounding my parents' farm, collecting wild flowers. I loved the beautiful king cup—a giant buttercup that likes boggy soil—and the delicate yellow patches of the dainty cowslips that appeared in early spring on the field where the cows were put out to graze.

I still love the smell of hawthorn blossom in early May and recall the shedding pollen of the rye grass and cow parsley, several feet tall, that made me sneeze each May and June around exam time. Modern farming techniques have lumped these wildflowers together under the heading of weeds and have sprayed some of them to near extinction.

Fortunately, many are now protected in England where I live, and it is illegal to pick them for fear of wiping out this beautiful heritage. But, as the old saying goes, a weed is a flower by any other name, and some wildflowers are more magical than the fanciest hybrid bloom.

At a very young age I became aware of many of the superstitions and the folklore surrounding the flowers of field and hedgerow. For instance, I knew that it was thought to be unlucky to pick and bring inside the mayflower or the heavenly scented white lilac. Dark green foliage such as holly and mistletoe were considered to have a pagan ancestry. Because of this, people only brought them indoors at Christmas, when there was enough goodwill around to ward off any evil spirits lurking in them.

As a child I was also fascinated by the climbing dog roses and old, wild sweet peas that curled through the tangled undergrowth, and I soon began to realize that whenever a flower was picked, the dying process began. It was not long before I knew that the delicate red field poppy would barely survive a day, while the perfectly formed oxeye daisy would brave wind and rain and if picked would last for days in clean water. This was the start of my natural philosophy of flower arranging. Only long-lasting specimens should be harvested. Those with shorter lives were better dug up and transformed into miniature growing gardens with moss and constant watering to help them along.

Each season brought fresh delights—a feeling I have tried to retain in my flower arranging. In late summer, white achillea and delicious scented meadowsweet combined to bring each day to a fragrant end, while the landscape began to change to a richly textured mix of vines and seed heads. Wheat and barley fields turned from green to gold, then overnight were harvested and laid bare once more, making the flowers that remained in the landscape all the more precious. By winter, all these had turned into berries, seed heads and fruits, presenting the flower arranger with another range of possibilities. There were the juice-laden elderflower berries, the purple sloe berries, and squidgy, round pearlized berries of the snowberry bush. The dog rose bore wonderful red hips, which made me itch terribly. Unfriendly blackberry bushes scratched any predator, while the glorious fluffy seed heads of the wild clematis, known as old man's beard, added further mystery to the now-gray hedgerows. As their leaves fell, beautiful, strong deciduous trees took on graphic new shapes, bringing a different look to my familar landscape with its hill on the horizon.

And so, surrounded throughout my childhood by the countryside and constantly exposed to nature and the changing seasons, it is not surprising that I found my inspiration here. It was not long before I became fascinated by flower arranging and mesmerized by the variety of colors, textures, and shapes of the individual blooms.

From an early age I would arrange my collections of flowers simply and informally in small pots and vases, experimenting with pre-florist's foam mechanics such as pinholders, rose-bowl grids, and heavy glass weights with holes to hold stems. I anchored crumpled chickenwire in ceramic pots and learned to cut and position stems. One of the wonderful things about arranging flowers is that although specialized equipment is available, it is not essential, so this is one hobby you can start without the need for expensive capital outlay.

It was also during my childhood that I realized the value of foliage. Once you experiment with it, you soon start to see how green acts as a color control for other flowers.

If you have a hot collection of colors, you need heavy, dark foliage to give the arrangement balance. Dark or dull color schemes call for acid-green, variegated, or silver foliages to lighten them up. Pale and pastel colors require careful foliage selections that do not overshadow them or make them appear insipid.

I quickly discovered that the easiest way to make a room look cared for, fresh, and alive was to add a simple flower arrangement. It beat housework any day. But a simple arrangement is not always as effortless as it appears. Making ten gerberas in a vase look stunning requires concentration and time. The trick for producing truly simple flowers is to make sure your plant material is chosen for its clever combination of color, texture, and shape, that it looks natural, and that the flowers are positioned absolutely perfectly.

I don't know anyone who is not in awe of the beauty of flowers. They are truly to be treasured. With their simple elegance, they have proved a fascination for centuries. And although I am surrounded by flowers every day, I am amazed by their continuing ability to astonish, amuse, and enthrall me. I hope the simple arrangements in this book will inspire you to transform your living and working spaces with some of this beauty.

Here a simple highball glass has been put into service as a vase in a bathroom with a seaside theme. The chincherinchees are robust and can withstand the atmospheric changes associated with bathrooms. They lean toward the light, so turn them regularly.

single flowers

As orientals have observed, to contemplate a single bloom can be more nourishing to the soul than to see a mass of flowers, however stunning they may be.

Every single bloom is made up of many different parts, each of which contributes to its total, exquisite beauty. This can best be appreciated when that bloom is seen on its own. Then it becomes a living work of art—like a sculpture to be viewed and wondered at from every different angle.

The famous architect Mies van der Rohe is credited with two of the most overused design edicts: "Less is more," and "God is in the details." These apply as much to the flower arranger as to a designer or architect, since to study one single bloom can be far greater food for the soul than to observe a mass of flowers. Some single blooms are so beautiful that they require nothing more of the arranger than to be well conditioned and placed in a suitable container. When I am working in my flower shop, I am most intrigued by the customer who buys one single bloom, for to me the gift of just one exquisite flower can be more poignant than armfuls of expensive blooms. In short, a single flower can say it all.

When you observe a single bloom, you become much better acquainted with it and with the many parts of it that contribute to its exquisite beauty: the pattern on its leaves, the texture and arrangement of its petals, the color of its stem, the shape of its calyx and corolla, its distinctive scent. With a single bloom arrangement you can capitalize on just one of these features. The first camellia of spring is one of my special pleasures. Its flower is stunningly beautiful, but equally glorious are its waxy, green leaves. Make the most of them by placing the flower in a small vase, its dainty face surrounded by a collar of leaves. I also like to exploit scented flowers by using them as single specimens. One simple gardenia flower floating in a bowl of fresh water with candles makes a sensuous focal point on a dresser, while an old-fashioned, heavenly scented garden rose sitting by your bed at night is sure to guarantee sweet dreams. Similarly, a beautifully scented carnation floating in a fingerbowl at a place setting brings fragrance for each guest at a dinner party. A single branch of spring blossom or a bough of autumn berries evokes the season, while in my own home, one of my most favored single flowers is the phalaenopsis orchid, which I love for its exquisite shape.

top row from left to right A stem of 'Radiant Queen' Guernsey lilies stands in a chunky earthenware bottle; 'Jedi Spider Roze' and 'Jedi Spider Yellow' gerberas are arranged with yellow achillea and peach 'Medea' carnations massed at the base of their stems in florist's foam in diamond-shaped, ceramic pots; a blood flower looks regal in a classical-shaped, glazed black vase; mini 'Sonja' sunflower plants have been planted into small galvanized pots with orange-sprayed gravel covering the soil; a single scarlet 'Red Garnet' dahlia makes a perfect specimen; one pincushion flower in a striped, ceramic cylinder vase makes a bold statement.
second row from left to right A lone orange Iceland poppy has a delicate fragility; a favorite perfume bottle supports a dainty stem of bearded wheat; its exposed bulb and root system give this 'Red Lion' amaryllis a contemporary feel.

15

this page clockwise The amaryllis bulb produces enormous and dramatic blooms from compact buds. Some varieties have such large flowers that the hollow stems need to be supported with canes or, as an interesting alternative, with contorted willow. I love the variegated markings of this particular family member—'Minerva'; frosted glass containers are versatile for both contemporary and traditional locations; a faded terra-cotta vase echoes the hint of color in these 'Moon' tulips; a single head of papyrus supports four 'Lothario' flag irises in each of these opaque, lilac flutes.

opposite page The timeless elegance of lily vases transforms a few stems of lilies into a sculptural feature. Lily pollen stains, so it is best to remove the five stamens by simply pinching them out. Wash your hands immediately. If you accidentally brush pollen onto your clothes, carefully dab the mark with tape until it disappears. The lily pictured here is 'Casa Blanca.'

16

When you position one flower in a vase, you have to think more about the arrangement in terms of shape and height. Approach it as you might a piece of art or sculpture. Think at what height and from what direction it is best viewed, then arrange it to show it off to best advantage. Take care to place it where it will be most complemented and look naturally perfect. In short, be impassioned and creative.

One bonus of single-flower arrangements is that they can be quick to achieve and inexpensive. One simple bloom in a guest bedroom shows that you care without being extravagant. A beautiful nerine on a breakfast tray can make an everyday meal into a statement of affection.

A single stem of freesia or of scented narcissus, or a lone hyacinth, are perfect to freshen your bathroom. In winter I love the sensuous pleasure of having a hyacinth growing in my bathroom to fragrance my bath times.

If you do not have hours to spare constructing flower displays but want to use flowers in your own home, then single-flower arrangements are for you. All you need is to start making a collection of the perfect vases for single flowers, then you are well on the way to filling your house with flowers at the least cost and greatest speed.

One or two flowers in glass test tubes or in plastic phials will add something special to any interior. Another lovely way of displaying single flowers is to place them in low bowls or tall glasses. A few beautiful glass goblets at different heights, filled with rose heads and arranged on a silver tray in the middle of a table, have a very striking classical appeal. If the flower is just resting on the top of the water, the effect of the refraction creates a very interesting impression. Poppies can be treated in a similar way, staggered at different heights across a modern dining table. Carefully singe the ends of each stem, then place in a single-flower container of your choice and arrange in a line down the middle of the table.

Completely submerging a flower in water also makes a wonderful focal point for a dinner party. The flower can be weighted down in a tall glass vase or placed in a pinholder at the base. Soon masses of tiny air bubbles will appear around the flower as oxygen surfaces from the water. This all adds to the beauty of the whole effect.

Foliage can also look great on its own. Even a single unusual leaf such as a swiss-cheese leaf or a handful of beargrass or horsetail can make an interior look fresh. Or you could try making a table runner from stalks of snakegrass bound together with fine wire or plastic thread.

One of my favorite foliage-based dinner-table ideas is to dress a long table with a richly colored tablecloth and to place a long vine of ivy down the middle, adding the occasional exotic flower. One terrific flower to use is the lotus flower, a mysterious and temperamental specimen from tropical and

left The Eucharis lily has the purest white star-shaped flowers with fresh green centers and a delicate scent. Originating in South America, the Eucharis lily is also often referred to as the Amazon lily.
right Stems of curly pancho reed have been sprayed gold and twine themselves sinuously around two conical frosted vases of Eucharis lilies.

below Plant pots have been painted cream to complement the deep orange color of the mass of 'Little Sun' alstroemerias.

right A cluster of orange-toned zinnias have been tightly tied beneath their heads so the tie is concealed, and then securely placed in florist's foam in a white-painted pot. To finish the arrangement, the foam is covered with moss. The effect is one of a topiary tree.

subtropical regions that comes in beautiful shades of pink and white.

Tease the flowers open by placing in a deep basin of water in direct sunlight. Place the open blooms in phials of water, which you conceal by covering with double-sided tape and large flexible ivy leaves. Hide the covered phials in the ivy vine on your table, dotting the flowers down the length of the table. In addition, you could place one lotus bloom on each plate for your guests to take home. In their natural habitat, lotus flowers close in the evening, so this arrangement is best attempted for a summer lunchtime celebration.

left Filling a container with a mass of one type of flower as in this horizontal arrangement of arum lilies always creates maximum impact and is the way I prefer to arrange flowers in my own home. Cutting the stems short and just having the flower heads peeping over the rim of the container often suits trumpet-shaped flowers such as arum lilies and globe-shaped, petaled flowers like dahlias, as well as flowers borne on inflorescences such as alstroemerias.
below The black noses on the white faces of these stars of Bethlehem mirror the black and white checked pots to give this design a graphic feel.

Other tropical flowers, such as the elegant and strangely textural flowers of the banana family, can also look very striking laid sparingly on top of leaves for a table decoration. In fact, tropical flowers and foliage lend themselves especially well to single-flower arrangements. Perhaps it is because, for most of us, their exotic, eye-catching beauty is an unfamiliar sight. Used in single-specimen arrangements—and for reasons of expense, that is often desirable—we have the opportunity to admire and wonder at them without interference from other, extraneous material. They will last well, especially in hot weather when temperate flowers will quickly give up, but unfortunately they do not wither and fade gently and beautifully as our traditional flowers do, but suddenly rot and turn a nasty blackish-brown. Tropical flowers such as the bird-of-paradise flower from Australia and California, celosia and heliconia from the Caribbean, scarlet plume from Mexico, anthuriums from the West Indies, and proteas from South Africa need little to enhance their breathtaking colors and forms except, perhaps, some dark green foliage.

The best bold foliage is often the tropical sort. On its own, it too can make a very powerful statement. New Zealand flax has striking sword-shaped broad leaves edged with reddish-orange. Papyrus grass—depicted together with lotus flowers in ancient Egyptian tomb painting—has whorls of bright green leafy bracts that can be trimmed into crisp, geometric shapes. Banana leaves are deep green and broad with distinct horizontal ribs, while the palms range from the relatively small fan palm to the gigantic Canary Island date palm.

A variation on the single-flower theme can involve arranging a mass of the same flower in a single vase or in several small vases. This is a very enduring look that works best when you use flowers in season.

Then they are at their most inexpensive and you can afford to use enough of them to make a bold, generous display. A mass of tulips or narcissi arranged without any other adornment at spring time is a real delight after the harsh days of winter, while a display of blowsy rose heads conjures up a real sense of a summer garden at the height of its glory.

Some flowers, such as the sweet peas pictured here, actually look best on their own. That is because their complicated shape makes it difficult to find other flowers that work well with them. Even foliage can often look incongruous and over-fussy.

One especially attractive way of arranging a mass of the same specimens in a vase is to use a horizontal arrangement, as in the display of arum lilies on the previous page. This look particularly suits long dining tables, console tables in halls, or grand mantelpieces. It is very popular with many of the top floral designers. In it the flowers are teased and tussled to coax them into shape in the vase. The mystery is in the making!

opposite, left and above Like many people who were lucky enough to have spent their childhood in the country, one of the first flowers I wanted to cultivate were sweet peas. Their divine scent and magnificent array of colors guarantee their position in my premier league of flowers. Sadly, home-grown sweet peas do not last very long but the commercially grown varieties are chemically treated after harvesting to guarantee their longevity as cut flowers. There is no better way to see sweet peas than massed together, and they look particularly stunning in these clear glass vases like ice-cream sundae glasses. Together they are the epitome of idyllic summer days.

mixing flowers

Flowers that work well together in mixed arrangements are a delight to the eye, each specimen enhancing and complementing the beauty of its companions.

But mixing flowers is the hardest skill for a flower arranger to learn. Only experience will help you find the perfect combinations. From using different varieties of flower in a single color or range of tones, you will gradually become confident enough to experiment in a more daring fashion.

Single colors are strong and simple, so they are often the choice of interior designers and architects who like them because of the way they underline rather than detract from the qualities of their designs. Making a bold, clear, undiluted statement, they often suit interiors decorated in strong colors, like the dark-blue-painted room shown here. But using single colors does not mean that you have to stick to a single variety of flower. By mixing the varieties but matching the color, you can double the impact and interest. And with the constant arrival on the market of new varieties of flowers and foliage, you will always have plenty of material, even when you are attempting to work within the confines of a single color.

White is the classic color of flower arranging. It combines with any other color and is a good choice for novice flower arrangers who may be afraid to use stronger colors. Here white flowers are used for a classic blue-with-white, but that statement has been given a new twist, thanks to the unexpected choice of flowers. In truly modern style, *Ammi majus* flowers peep coyly out over the top of the elegant silver-toned vase, while tall chincherinchees act as a counterpoise to the weight of the vase.

I have always loved color and one of the most exciting aspects of working with cut flowers is the endless opportunity it presents for finding new color combinations. The palette is constantly changing. Nearly every week I see a new variety of flower at Covent Garden, London's famous flower market, and this often presents new color combination possibilities. Similarly, if I am traveling in a part of the world I have not previously visited, I sometimes have the chance to work with different plant materials. With such immense diversity there is always something new for me to try.

You can learn a lot from studying color wheels and color theory, and gardening and interior decoration books are full of information about how these work, but to my mind nothing succeeds like practice. You will find that working with flowers has a lot to do with color balance and the use of green as a regulator. I often think of the color green as being like the device on a television that controls the color. The right green in the right combination makes any color combination perfect. The wrong green, or not enough of it, will be death to the arrangement.

opposite and this page The arrangements pictured here are monochromatic. They use shades and tones of similar colors—pinks, blues, whites, and creams, and deep violets. Working within a restricted palette like this can make it simpler to achieve displays with plenty of impact.

The versatility of wood offers the flower arranger all kinds of inspiring possibilities. It comes in many colors, depending on the wood, and can be used in its rough, untreated state, as here, or varnished or polished for a richer look. An arrangement like this one would make an unusual choice for a wedding or christening table centerpiece. The pale colors are the perfect foil for the untreated wood. Other containers with a natural feel that would suit flowers in this color range include trugs, old barrels, or ethnic baskets, which come in a host of shapes, sizes, and weaves. Alternatively, you could adapt a piece of tree trunk, bark, or driftwood picked up during a country or seaside walk. And if you do not have any of these, you could try covering any straight-sided container such as a jar or plastic box with double-sided tape, and attaching to it twigs, sticks, or pieces of bamboo cut to even-sized lengths.

boxed in

Line an untreated box or basket of your choice with heavy-duty plastic sheeting. **Soak** some florist's foam by putting it in a bucket of water. **Fill** the lined container with the soaked foam, cut to fit. **Cut** the stems of the roses, pinks, alstroemeria, lisianthus, and lady's mantle down to about 2 inches and remove any leaves, then position in the florist's foam. **Arrange** the flowers in groups so that they have greater impact. **Dot** with the snowberries. **Fill** in any gaps with clusters of attractive foliage to give a dome-shaped arrangement. You can fill with variegated pittosporum and mind-your-own-business as I have, or you could use moss.

Flowers:

3 rose heads
1 bunch 'Doris' pinks
1 bunch pale pink alstroemeria
2 stems pale pink lisianthus
3 stems lady's mantle
1 sprig snowberry
3 sprigs variegated pittosporum
Mind-your-own-business, to fill

opposite, far right and right Nature is endlessly resourceful and provides us not just with flowers, but also with foliage and vegetables from which to draw inspiration. In this clay-pot arrangement of flowers, foliage, herbs, and vegetables, the dominant color is green. The succes of monochromatic designs like this relies as much on contrasting and complementary textures as on shades and tones. Here, subtly varied shades of green are present in graphic-shaped tulips, scallions, galax leaves, and green-and-white 'Tinkerbell' arum lilies, in the lacy heads of dill and snow-on-the-mountain, and in the rounded heads of creamy green lisianthus and of guelder rose. The finishing touch is provided by a variegated spurge.

pale colors

Pale colors go in and out of fashion, but for religious events and serious occasions they are often preferred. The delicacy, translucency, and fragility of colors such as pink, peach, and lilac give immense pleasure, while white is often considered pure and divine. Whereas pure color tends to be confrontational, pastel colors beguile with their sensitivity and subtlety.

White flowers are the classic choice to give when you do not know someone's personal taste or the style of their home. The subtle blue of love-in-the-mist, with its highly textured tendrils, makes a cool color for summer interiors or for summer brides. Scabious, with its pincushion centers of white and blue, has an almost childlike innocence. Humble scented narcissi with their contrasting spring-green stems look pure and clean with their heads all massed together in a simple vase. The unashamed beauty of some of the palest Parrot tulips as they float over the edge of a container in search of more light is an irresistible, ever-changing feast for the eyes.

The natural beauty of pale flowers can be enhanced with an astute choice of foliage such as pale elaeagnus, eucalyptus, and *Brachyglottis* 'Sunshine.' Delicately shaped flowers like starry astrantia or the much-maligned but still beautiful miniature white balls of baby's breath also combine well with pastel flowers. They will not overwhelm the softness of the pastel shades in the way that more solid-looking accompaniments would. Another stunning combination with delicate colors is cow parsley or Queen Ann's lace, which has beautiful, floaty umbrella-shaped flowerets. Pale colors also work well with the whiff of herbs, so try them with frothy green aromatic dill, or put pale lavender alongside sage and rosemary.

In the world of pale flowers, the beautiful phalaenopsis orchid is a real star. With its exotic shape and the range of ethereal colors it offers, it brings a hint of magic to any interior or function. If it were a person, it would be the perfect guest, always able to fit in with everyone and make polite conversation. As a cut flower, it is long lasting, either for an arrangement or in a bridal bouquet. Planted, it works well in all kinds of container and looks as splendid in an eighteenth-century foyer as it does in a loft apartment.

The increasing development of new colors by orchid growers makes the phalaenopsis orchid even more versatile. The white varieties are so bright that they are the purest white flowers grown and are the perfect choice if pure white is what you are looking for. The cream and spotted varieties go well with oyster and vanilla colors. These are the most popular, but for the really daring there are bright purplish-pink sprays that shriek for attention and are a great choice for contemporary arrangements.

Orchids make up one of the largest families in the plant kingdom, encompassing as many as 20,000 species. In the wild, they are quite hardy and can be found growing in some very inhospitable places. In the nineteenth century, they were highly sought for their exquisite beauty. Orchid hunters often risked their lives to collect rare examples, so the flowers came to be associated with romance and excitement.

It is not surprising, then, that orchids have always been considered a luxury. Now grown commercially, they are, in fact, one of the most time-consuming cut flowers to produce. The commercially grown varieties can take up to six years before they start bearing blooms. Each plant rarely flowers for more than five years and produces only about four stems of flowers a year. Unsurprisingly, growers are continually searching for ways of improving the performance of their plants in order to maximise their revenue potential. As a result of this quest, the art of orchid growing has evolved into a science, and the larger specialist nurseries now have on-site laboratories.

left and above The phalaenopsis orchid is so exquisitely beautiful that it is at its best on its own. All it takes to make an arrangement is a row of clear glass vases positioned on a long dining table or low occasional table, as here. Just add two or three stems to each vase and fill to the same level with water. The result is the epitome of simple chic. The soft color contrasts of the different varieties add a touch of sparkle to the arrangement, without detracting from its feeling of calm tranquility. You can achieve a similar effect using other flowers with interesting shapes. I would suggest trying lilies, Singapore orchids, arum lilies, sandersonia, or chincherinchees.

left Three simple vases of gerberas give a taste of the stunning hot colors that are possible. The simple daisylike form of the gerbera and its myriad colors, sizes, and textures have made it today's most popular flower. It comes in hundreds of varieties, with the result that growers nowadays are concentrating only on developing those strains that last for three weeks or more as cut flowers.

hot colors

I love hot colors. Because they appear to advance towards the eye, they are always spectacularly striking and vibrant. Clustered or grouped together, they are at their most dynamic and dramatic. The hot color range allows you to demonstrate your creative flair to the very limit.

Hot desert and Mediterranean landscapes suit hot colors perfectly. Sunshine takes all the life out of delicate shades, but hot colors are vital and energizing, and are not so easily defeated.

If you are planning to bring hot-colored flowers into your home, bear in mind that they look best either in very bright or in rather dark interiors. In a sparkling, sun-filled location, their zest becomes yet another element in the whole.

Yellow—the color of the sun—is one of the hottest colors, radiating warmth wherever it goes. Many of the yellows are referred to as gold shades and will add depth and richness to any interior. Among my favorite yellows are the bright yellow of the French marigold and the buttery yellow of the spring ranunculus.

In late summer I love the hot, yellow achillea flowers that dwarf the perennial borders of the garden, and I enjoy mixing it with orange red-hot pokers, steely blue globe thistles, and sea holly. Goldenrod and sunflowers are other yellow flowers that will add drama to an arrangement.

Bergenia cordifolia 'Purpurea' are both excellent examples. Dark red roses and dahlias also often have very dark foliage that enhances their richly colored petals beautifully. *Rosa* 'Black Magic' and *Dahlia* 'Bishop of Llandaff' are two of these.

Because it falls between red and yellow on the color wheel, orange is at the core of the hot colors. Think of the intensity of nasturtiums, marigolds, and Iceland poppies.

Hot color schemes are perfect for cooler dark days and I find that people are instinctively drawn to these combinations in the fall.

This is a time to combine dark red with attention-seeking orange. Try using Chinese lanterns with red-hot poker or torch lily. I also cannot resist the red fruits of the 'John Downie' crab apple or the berries of 'Orange Glow' firethorn.

above Blocks of *Rosa serena* in hot colors appear to burst out of their classical cream-colored urn. Grouping contrasting masses of flowers together adds impact to the overall design and is a good way of making unusual or contrasting color combinations work effectively. By choosing a container in a traditional style and color such as this one, it becomes easier to bridge the gap between hotly energetic flowers and coolly classical interiors.
above right Mini gerberas and ranunculi are also arranged in blocks of contrasting colors, this time in a basket.

Red is the color that is supposed to stop us in our tracks so it has come to symbolize "stop." We supposedly see red when we are mad and paint the town red when we have a wild night out. Red is the color of danger and therefore the color of drama and excitement, too.

Bright red flowers look sensational with dark red foliage, and often nature gives us this combination in one plant. The dark red *Lobelia cardinalis* 'Queen Victoria' and the strong-leafed

hot & spicy

This arrangement uses a brightly colored woven-grass container, but any container will do.

Line a container with plastic sheeting and fill with soaked florist's foam. **Arrange** the papyrus, clusters of ranunculi and roses, dill and dendranthemums. **Dot** with fern and photinia foliage. **Fold** the flax leaves and slip between the flowers, then add the ting-ting and sweet gale.

Flowers:

5 stems papyrus

15 red ranunculi

9 'Orange Unique' roses

3 *Dendranthemum* 'Shamrock'

7 stems dill

5 stems light-green fern

7 stems *Photinia* 'Red Robin'

10 stems New Zealand flax

1 bunch ting-ting reed

1 bunch sweet gale

unusual colors

I was recently invited to a convention of interior designers and members of related industries. One of the speakers said that it had never occurred to her to put cerise and orange together. It would never occur to me not to put these colors, or indeed any others, together.

To my mind, you can combine any colors you want as long as you are brazen and do it boldly. Color combinations that do not look good have simply not been thought through.

Whenever a new variety of flower or foliage appears—and that is often one a week—the possibility of a new color combination is born. For me, new additions are part of the excitement of my work. For example, I like to take a safe color like peach and add drama to it by mixing it with some of the newer dark colors such as blue and maroon. Treated in this way, peach immediately ceases to be insipid and takes on a whole new personality.

Drab colors such as the brownish red of vines and the plum of love-lies-bleeding can be difficult for the flower arranger and often require masses of fluffy acid green, like lady's mantle or the guelder rose, to make them come alive. In fact, lime green is now an important color for flowers, so hybridizers are hard at work trying to produce green dendranthemums and carnations, and are attempting to extend the season of acid-green plant material.

Bells of Ireland have been an essential green for flower arranging since the beginning of the twentieth century. Their pale green enhances any scheme, and their erect habit gives all-important height. A shell-shaped calyx surrounds each of the small white flowers that grow in clusters the length of the stem, providing rich texture as well. The green *Zinnia* 'Envy' is a personal favorite of mine, and I love green hellebores for the punch they can add to arrangements in late spring.

left A vase consisting of linked test tubes is filled with roses in clashing colors.
far left Colored chemical flasks filled with roses in unusual mixed colors are positioned on a reflective surface to double their impact. Several small arrangements like these dotted around on low tables instead of a single formal display produce a more contemporary effect and leave time and space for the good things in life, such as a glass or two of wine!

Flowers in classic combinations such as blue with white, or pink with cream, work well on their own. But If you wish to experiment with color and perhaps combine two unlikely partners, remember that plenty of dark green foliage can keep the warring factions at bay and make the marriage work successfully.

You could start by looking to nature for inspiration. The orange and purple of the bird-of-paradise flower is one exciting combination. Or think of art and study the flower paintings of the old Flemish and Dutch schools, whose dark backgrounds make the vibrant colors of the fruit, flower, and insect life in them sing out. Monet and Van Gogh, and, more recently, Georgia O'Keeffe are among those who have made me take a fresh look at color combinations.

left and above I cannot resist the majestic combination of red and purple no matter what the context. Arranged in a golden urn, this rich formal design is given a lift with a splash of lime-green guelder roses.
right Here, concentric circles of deep rose-colored pinks and lilac alliums make an attractive, simple-to-achieve modern arrangement.

proportion

A design needs to be in proportion to its surroundings in order to create the required effect, so scale is a very important factor.

One large arrangement will stand out more in a room full of people or in a double-height space than a multitude of small ones. Scale is also important when you come to choosing a container and making sure it will suit the plant material it is to hold.

In traditional floristry it was always recommended that an arrangement be one-and-a-half times taller than its container. This was rather limiting, but now the rule has been broken, and contemporary flower arrangers only use it when it suits them. Today's fashion for placing flowers just above the top of a vase with little or no stem showing is very untraditional. This trend was started at the Paris fashion shows of designer Christian Lacroix, but is now *de rigueur* everywhere.

Playing tricks with scale can create amusing arrangements that make us stop and stare. For example, you could take small flowers, such as violets, grape hyacinths, or snowdrops, and instead of using them sparingly in tiny vases as their size might ordinarily dictate, mass them together to create sumptuous, over-the-top arrangements. Similarly, you can remove the heads from giant sunflowers and float them in huge bowls of water filled with gray-toned pebbles. Another eye-catching play on scale can be achieved by placing a few tall flowers among groups of short ones.

45

small arrangements

If, like mine, your home has high ceilings and is sparsely furnished, it can be the ideal setting for large, really bold arrangements. However, on table tops or shelves, I love to use a number of small, sometimes miniature designs. They make a superb, strong contrast to the large displays in the room, each one serving to emphasize the size and scale of the other.

Tiny containers that were originally intended to serve a kitchen purpose, such as egg cups or spice jars, are amusing for undersized, Alice-in-Wonderland arrangements in eating areas. Fill them with brightly colored auriculas, pansies, or anemones. For maximum effect, dot them along the length of a dining table where they will add a bit of fun and color to the occasion.

If you want a pint-sized arrangement for a bathroom or breakfast tray, or to say a special thank-you to someone, you could try using small, empty perfume bottles filled with delicate flowers such as snowdrops, lily of the valley, grape hyacinths, or violets.

Many of the Danish, Dutch, and Belgian plant growers are now specializing in producing new miniature varieties of well-known plants, scarcely more than 4 inches tall, which are the ideal choice for this type of container. Tiny margarita daisies or miniature gerberas planted in diminutive pots last longer than cut flowers and make delightful gifts for dinner-party guests to take home with them.

Some flowers, such as lotus flowers and gardenias, are so exquisite that a single head is all you need to make a beautiful miniature arrangement. In countries of the East, gardenia blooms are often floated in bowls of tea to impart a delicate flavor to the drink. This idea has inspired me to float gardenia heads in a bowl of water, together with some floating candles. The result is an exquisite, perfumed centerpiece

far left Sinuously exotic mango-colored arum lilies and matching pincushion flowers make a bold but small-scale grouping on a side table with tropical-looking epipremnum and pandanus leaves.

left 'Golden Apeldoorn' tulips peep over the top of a lime-green glass while stems of snakegrass elbow their way through to try and steal the show.

top Mini margaritas planted in tiny zigzag-edged pots would brighten up any spring day, particularly at Easter.

above Single gardenia flowers look and smell heavenly in tiny ramekins of various colors dotted over a table top.

right A row of pots is painted to match mini gerbera plants. The repeating motif of small pots and plants makes a long-lasting architectural statement on top of this plinth.

far left Pebbles spray-painted silver lift a simple glass container out of the ordinary and provide support for a tightly packed bunch of dahlias.
center left Tie an ivy leaf with raffia to the front and back of a collection of ordinary jam jars, and use them to hold posies of 'Pinkie' bachelor's buttons. This arrangement demonstrates how a collection of small containers can make a big impact.
left Six stems of 'Cote d'Azure' freesias are held in florist's foam in a wedge-shaped aluminum container. The foam is disguised with overlapping leaves of flax.
below left Blue bachelor's buttons cut all to the same length stand in a galvanized pot with florist's foam.

for a dinner-party table. Dinner-party guests might also appreciate a tiny sweet-scented posy of violets edged with their own leaves, or a small bundle of aromatic lavender tied with twine sitting at their place setting. At the end of the evening, they can take their little gifts home.

Rounded flowers such as dahlias and bachelor's button suit small-scale arrangements that are dome-shaped or flat and symmetrical. Their massed heads give a satisfying feeling of geometry and density. A wedge-shaped aluminum container makes the most of the abstract shape of a few freesias and draws attention to them in a way that a more traditional vase would not.

Small-scale arrangements are great for making the most of flowers that are plentiful and in season. To emphasize the abundance of the plant material, try grouping your tiny arrangements in clusters of three. This repetition is a very effective means of underlining a design.

If you are looking for an unusual arrangement for a long table in a modern setting, for instance, in an office conference room, you could try filling three identical small glass pots with the same flowers, and joining them together with pieces of cane, or you could lay three shallow, white porcelain ashtray-sized dishes along the table, and fill them with clumps of bright green moss for a very fresh-looking effect. For a Christmas table, try three miniature Christmas trees made of dried bay leaves attached to a conical base of florist's foam. In all these arrangements, the important thing is to keep it simple, using just one type of flower or foliage. Small-scale mixed arrangements simply don't have the same punch as single-flower or single-foliage small-scale displays. They just look busy.

top and right Aptly nicknamed "elephant's ears," these anthuriums together with contorted willow make a larger-than-life arrangement that richly deserves its unique container and stand. If you want to extend the life of contorted willow indefinitely, simply remove its leaves.
above Dark purplish-brown stems of *Fritillaria pinardii* make a stunning sight in their huge pumice-stone bowl in an all-white room. A handful of large pebbles conceals the florist's foam that anchors the stems. The finished effect looks completely natural. It is as if the fritillaries are growing in the wild.

left The blossom of the ornamental cherry ideally reflects the minimalist, even Japanese, style of this location, while the material of the container effectively echoes the surrounding stonework.

below Massed hydrangea heads in a classic pink, blue, and white combination give a great sense of structure. With its container covered in olive twigs to echo the stems of the ornamental cherry, the arrangement has become the focal point in this room.

large arrangements

Spring is a great time for creating large arrangements. The bare stems and branches of trees that have lain dormant through the winter are suddenly covered with fresh green shoots and flower buds. Cherry, plum, and apple blossom all come into flower and lend their delicate color to any room, modern or traditional,

while large tubs of anthuriums, hydrangeas, and fritillaries are perfect if you want to make a bold statement in a huge space. These large-scale floral displays require heavy pots and containers. I find many of mine at craft fairs and art galleries. Most are one-off pieces and so add to the uniqueness of the arrangement. The larger

the arrangement, the more important it is for the container to be attractive in its own right. In large spaces, freestanding floral displays take on the function of a sculpture. You can use any large container, either standing a smaller one inside to hold the water—essential if the display container is porous—or, for an arrangement in florist's foam, lining it with heavy plastic sheeting to keep the water from leaking out on your furniture or floor.

shape

Some plants are tall and spiky, while others grow into rounded domed shapes. Some develop along asymmetric and apparently misshapen lines, while others end up looking clean and linear. When garden designers are planning a garden, they are always very conscious of the shape plants make. I like to apply the same thinking to my flower arranging, so I always want to know how a plant grows in its natural habitat. Only then can I see the foliage that suits it and the colors that go with it. If you look only at the flower and not at the shape and symmetry of the whole plant, you miss out on one of the most important elements.

As plants grow and flower, a daily miracle of nature takes place. Take time to meditate on their form and contemplate the changes they will make tomorrow. Light-sensitive flowers especially continue to grow and move. Fritillaries will shift toward the sun and "spit" at you from

their flowerets. Tulips often confound you. In a mixed arrangement they might try to race away from the rest of the flowers, attempting to stand tall and always be king of the arrangement. At other times they droop; the heavily hybridized Parrot tulips are beautiful but have heads that are far too heavy for their weak, fleshy stems.

Some flowers are so bold that they are unsuitable for mixed arrangements. I think gladioli make such a wonderful shape on their own that they are done a great disservice when they are placed with other plant material. Often flowers like these have fallen from fashion because, in the past, they have been arranged badly or placed in unsuitable combinations. They do not suit posies and can look stiff in front-facing arrangements.

Longiflorum lilies are another example. They have been used for simple church arrangments for hundreds of years and look fabulous on their own. With their perfect simple green foliage they do not need any other accompaniment. They also provide an element of theater as they change from green buds to white trumpet shapes, revealing golden yellow stamens and releasing their divine scent.

above Arranged in a way that mimics the shape of their own flower heads, 'Royal Standard' red-hot pokers have a mass of *Achillea* 'Moonshine' positioned around the base of their stems.
right Show off two dozen 'Grand Prix' roses by making them into a soft dome shape using a piece of soaked florist's foam. They look effective in this contrasting blue triangular dish.
far right A dried-flower star brings some long-lasting fun to a kitchen windowsill. To make one, wrap a styrofoam star in strips of yellow tissue paper, then glue on dried heads of *Rudbeckia laciniata* to cover.

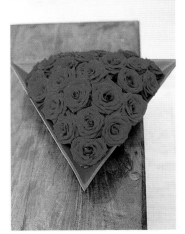

Other spire-shaped flowers like foxgloves, lupines, and foxtail lilies also have a strong sense of their own identity. I love them all. Each one of them will add a feeling of nobility and drama to an arrangement. Equally fascinating are the tall and perfectly straight stems of gayfeathers which, unlike other flowers, bloom from the top down. Most tall flowers, such as delphiniums, monkshood, and snapdragons, bloom in the opposite sequence.

There is a mystery to the contorted shape of some flowers and an intrigue about the way many of them are able to move into strange and convoluted positions as they grow. The red-hot poker is a popular flower with designer florists at the moment because it twists and moves in an interesting manner, and brings a feeling of life and movement to an arrangement. Some florists even like to wire and twist flowers into different shapes, but that is not my preferred style. I like to enjoy them in their natural state.

above, left and right To make these topiary-tree arrangements, hold the cut stems tightly in your hand to create a domed pompom shape. Tie together tightly just beneath the flower heads and insert them firmly in the foam-filled container. The white arrangement is made from 'Ludwig's Dazzler' amaryllis finished off with poppy seed heads around the base, while the orange arrangement consists of stems of clivia with red sand covering the foam.

right This double-ball topiary was made from a birch pole fixed in a pot using quick-setting cement. Heavy florist's wire holds two chicken-wire balls filled with moss to the pole. The balls were packed with wired-in gerbera heads and the cement was concealed with florist's foam studded with dried marigolds.

above left The unusual, almost synthetic appearance of anthuriums means that they combine well with highly graphic, stylized materials. Their rounded form makes a great contrast with anything spiky. Here I have used two varieties of anthurium with contorted willow.

above right The rounded shape of green 'Midori' and red 'Tropical' anthuriums contrasts with the broad spiky foliage of New Zealand flax. For a bit of fun, I put the red anthuriums in a yellow vase, and the green anthuriums in a red vase.

left Simple repetition and duplication of an arrangement has a calming effect that turns plant life into an interior design detail. Here I have placed three *Isolepis cernua* plants at the edge of a bath for tranquil bathtimes. I covered the plants' ugly plastic pots with snakegrass.

Whatever its shape, any flower or plant can make a striking contribution to an arrangement. Some, such as the pineapple flower, are wonderfully intriguing, while the fat, fleshy rosettes of leaves belonging to plants of the echeveria family provide some of the most pleasing shapes to be found.

The shape of the plant material will dictate the type of container. Generally speaking, long stems require tall containers, although recently the fashion has been for tall containers topped off with a mass of flower heads peeping over the rim. If you are brave, tall spiky arrangements can even be made in shallow bowls, as the photographs on page 52 show. Taking a lead from oriental floristry, material with an especially interesting shape looks best in the simplest of containers. In this way the container does not detract from the beauty of the flowers or foliage. It is also usually true that material with a strongly graphic shape looks best in plainer, contemporary containers.

birds-of-paradise

This tropical arrangement set against a red wall firmly puts the emphasis on the striking shapes of the flowers.

Fill an urn-shaped container with soaked florist's foam, ensuring that the foam is about 1 inch above the rim. **Trim** the stems of the flowers and foliage and remove any foliage from the lower part of the stems. **Arrange** the bird-of-paradise flowers and position the cardoons and pincushion flowers in clusters of three around their base. **Cover** any exposed florist's foam with the gaultheria and hebe foliage.

Flowers:
5 bird-of-paradise flowers
9 cardoons
9 pincushion flowers
Gaultheria and hebe foliage, to fill

texture

I cannot go past lambs' ears without wanting to stroke the fuzz that grows on the surface of their leaves, and like most people, I will avoid at any cost coming into contact with the sharp spikes of cacti. Gerberas are soft and downy, sea holly and globe thistles are prickly, and ranunculi—among my favorite flowers—have petals of the finest, most delicate texture that take on an ephemeral quality just before they fade. It is almost as if they are turning into wings before they fly off from the flowers, shattering into the most delicate confetti as they go.

The creative and imaginative interplay of textures is vital to modern floral design and is an element that anyone involved with flower arranging must consider. Just as you rarely dress in fabrics of only one texture, so you can bring life to an arrangement by the use of different textures of plant and other material.

Ten years ago, nearly every flower arrangement included a few sprays of fluffy white baby's breath as a filler. Now the trend is to use flowers with a more graphic texture—globular purple allium flowers or spiky chincherinchees. Berries, seed heads, and grasses also add texture, and each year brings a new fashion in these. The once-seasonal hypericum berry is now so popular that it is available fifty-two weeks a year.

Look carefully at what you use to see the contribution it can make—velvety celosia, the spiky yet soft fronds of pincushion flowers, and leathery evergreen laurel leaves are just a few examples. Notice how shiny surfaces leap out at you whereas matt surfaces recede and retire from view. Often, when I am working on flower photography, the photographer will start by taking a black-and-white Polaroid of my

59

I often find inspiration at the fruit and vegetable market. Clusters of grapes tumbling over the edge of an arrangement enhance with their soft, rounded gleam. Shiny red and green apples add bright color and subtle gloss.

Foliage offers some of the best textures. There are the slippery-looking leaves of camellia, holly, and gardenia. Gardenia is one of my favorite foliages. I love to use it for wedding work where its dark sheen enhances the creamy white of its charming, waxy flowers.

Feathery foliage presents other interesting textural opportunities. The frond-like vines of jasmine are perfect for wedding bouquets when the bride is dressed in soft organza. If she is in a heavier fabric, the stronger texture of stephanotis is a better choice.

The most textural plant material belongs to the family of cacti and succulents. The textural possibilities they offer range from waxy and smooth to hairy or spiny, and many also have the

above A twiggy frame is constructed for an arrangement of pale yellow gerberas using bunches of carnation stems. Strip the stems of their leaves to highlight their knobbly form. Massing flowers next to each other like this makes the textural contrast more intense.
above right Short lengths of horsetail provide an interesting disguise for the florist's foam holding a topiary arrangement in place.
right Using glass as a container automatically gives an arrangement another dimension. Here the angularity of the gravel is unexpectedly softened by the smooth glass and by the velvety texture and rounded leaves of the primulas.
far right I love pink, the brighter the better. This monochromatic arrangement in an unusual harmonizing pink container contrasts soft 'Pinkie' bachelor's buttons with pink-sprayed gravel, taking the flowers from the field to the next millenium.

arrangements. This gives me the opportunity to see how well the textural qualities are working without the distraction of color. Try, as I do, to think of an arrangement as if it were a piece of patchwork, with different textures creating blocks of depth and interest.

In fact, the best way to make bold textural arrangements for weddings, parties, and special occasions, is to place the flowers in large blocks so that the texture of one is played against that of the next. For these large-scale arrangements,

added bonus of brightly colored flowers. Their strong architectural appearance suits contemporary interiors, and they are also very forgiving of their owners, even if neglected for weeks at a time.

Be bold with your combinations of texture. I love the contrast of prickly sea holly and blue globe thistles with rounded, soft-looking summer blooms. I even mixed a small variety of sea holly with lilies of the valley, pale pink roses, and downy silvery *Brachyglottis* 'Sunshine' to make my own wedding bouquet. The soft iridescent gray hairs on the brachyglottis look fantastic next to baby pink or soft blue, whereas shiny, metallic-looking accompaniments, such as some of the white-variegated ivies, would appear harsh and uncomfortable.

The hard knobbly texture of bare winter twigs can look effective with the smoothly elegant arum lily; fluffy mosses look good with walnuts; shiny green laurel leaves make a superb contrast with tiny soft balls of yellow mimosa.

right Pompom moss is a rare import from the tropics. It has the texture of bun moss, but is harvested on short stems that make it perfect for providing structure at the base of vase arrangements. Here five bunches have been arranged around the base of twenty stems of chincherinchees.
center In some countries it is the tradition to make an Advent wreath with a candle to light on each Sunday leading up to Christmas. This square version using pink alliums and Mexican orange foliage gives a new twist to an age-old theme.
far right I designed this arrangement for an outdoor summer party. A glass vase is filled with 'Purple Sensation' alliums and harmonizing blue delphiniums. More alliums have been woven around the vase to create a living basket.

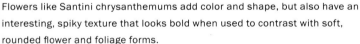

Flowers like Santini chrysanthemums add color and shape, but also have an interesting, spiky texture that looks bold when used to contrast with soft, rounded flower and foliage forms.

If you want to make an ordinary flower look special and give unexpected pleasure, then observe its texture and mix it with just a few exotic flowers or with plant material that has a different tactile quality. The rather dull autumn double chrysanthemum can prove surprising when mixed with the crisply textured leaves of ornamental cabbage or with smooth shiny gourds.

For something a bit different, try enhancing a flower or plant's texture with water. Sprinkle a few drops on a velvety rosebud and see how the surface of the petals is magnified, making its texture even richer. Or spray a mind-your-own-business plant with a fine mist. The plant's already highly tactile foliage will be irresistible to the touch once it sparkles with tiny droplets.

Don't forget, too, the plant material that is often thrown away, as well as foliage and inorganic material. Any of these can be used to add their magical texture to an arrangement. Carnation stems, for instance, have interesting nodules. These can be exploited to add a graphic feel to otherwise traditional flowers. Moss is the material you might first think of to conceal the florist's foam in an arrangement, but there are more original and lively textural possibilities. For instance, horsetail with its hollow, reedy stems. Cut sections of this can add the finishing touch to the florist's foam supporting a topiary tree. Gravel also makes a great alternative to moss in this type of situation, and can be used in its natural state or spray-painted in vibrant colors. Bark, shells, or stones are further possibilities. Each brings a different textural quality to an arrangement. Even humble sand can be used. Normally thought of as a rather dull brown, you can also find it in myriad colors, including stark black and white.

Some of the most interesting and simplest textural effects can be achieved by using plants with unusual growth habits. These are great fun and provide a more lasting display than cut flowers. The mound-forming herbs, such as the diminutive thyme—*Thymus serpyllum* 'Elfin,' with its minute, glossy rounded leaves—make a good choice. The very graphic echeverias, with their fleshy, succulent leaves that grow in rosettes would also be suitable, as would some of the low-growing kalanchoes. Many of these have leaves that turn from green to purple or red when they are exposed to light. That's an added enjoyment!

plants for textural effects

Flower pots Here I have taken three matching flower pots in pale green, pale blue, and yellowish-green and filled their bases with moss. I then planted a single bead plant with bright orange berries in each pot. The moisture-retentive moss will help to prevent the bead plant from drying out, but you could use crumpled newspaper or cellophane instead.

Blue star Mind-your-own-business is a great plant for arrangements because it is so versatile. It is very easy to maintain (regular watering is all that is required to keep it looking green and healthy,) and it will tolerate low light levels, so need not be placed near a window. It comes in varying shades of green, from pale gray-green to bright lime-green. Here I have used three different shades and simply planted them in a thin layer of soil-based potting mixture in a shallow star-shaped dish. The graphic shape of the dish is a perfect foil for the textured foliage.

You could also create an unusual and simple textural effect with a huge shallow bowl planted with lawn grass or moss. One of these makes a very striking centerpiece on a dark wooden table. It is like bringing a little of the outdoors into a room. To keep grass or moss bright green, remember to water regularly. Aside from that they are trouble-free.

Spanish moss, *Tillandsia usneoides*, is strictly speaking not a moss but a bromeliad, one of the so-called "air plants" without roots. It is a fascinating low-growing plant with gray, branching, wiry stems that you can grow on a piece of bark. It would look great alternating with clumps of bright green bun moss on top of a shallow glass dish.

For these displays, you will get the best effects by using containers in shapes that you wouldn't normally use for plants, and in colors that look well against the leaves. You can also try grouping your plants in pairs, threes, or fives. This makes an eye-catching display where a single plant might go unnoticed. Even rather old-fashioned specimens like mother-in-law's tongue can be strikingly contemporary set in a group of rectangular pots.

containers

Anyone who is serious about flower arranging needs a cupboard full of containers to choose from. The container can make or break an arrangement.

Glass is a clear winner, but do not ignore even the humble plastic bowl. With a bit of imagination, it can be transformed into a one-off container fit for the most stylish occasion. Or, for truly glamorous effects, try wrapping a simple vase in a lavish swathe of fabric selected to complement your choice of flowers.

glass

Glass is the most versatile material for holding flowers. I love the simplicity of stems in water. Glass containers reveal them completely, so that you get the sense of looking at the whole flower in growth.

But glass also provides a window of creative opportunity. With it you can add another dimension to any arrangement by putting the anchoring material on view as well. You can fill it with anything that takes your fancy. Try shells, stones, and even small fruits and vegetables to hold the flowers and foliage in place.

If you choose a toning filler to submerge in the body of the vase, the colorfulness of the entire arrangement will be doubled. Try small tomatoes, orange and lemon slices, small peppers, and berries. Such an arrangement is only suitable for a day or so though, as the plant material that is submerged in the water will quickly start to rot.

You can achieve a similar effect by placing the container holding the flowers inside a larger glass one, and filling the space between with decorative material. This is especially suited to material that you could not easily put in the water with the flowers, for instance potpourri, moss, or sand. If your container is too small or narrow to hold another one, you can place your flowers in small phials that can be purchased from florists' shops.

For small-scale arrangements of tiny posies of primroses or violets, I love to use drinking glasses or tumblers, or even champagne flutes. By contrast, if you are using a large glass vase with a wide opening—or any other large vase for that matter—make it more user friendly by

placing a grid of cellophane tape or florist's tape across the top. This will help to anchor the stems and stop them from flopping.

Glass comes in a wide variety of types and in the full range of designs, from classic to contemporary. Handblown glass, with all its imperfections and tiny bubbles, is attractive and can make flowers look as if they are in sparkling water. Frosted and opaque glass also make attractive containers. I especially like those that look as if they are made of ice.

If you are arranging flowers in a clear glass vase, the most important thing to remember is that the glass should be sparkling clean, so always dry it with a soft cloth each time you wash it. When clear, clean water starts to grow cloudy, the time has come to rinse out your container with diluted bleach and start again with fresh, tepid water and some flower food.

Finally, to make the most of glass containers, position them where the light will pass through and brighten up the display.

opposite Gerberas in phials of water stand in an unusual glass-fronted container full of crab apples.
above left Red peppers, slices of orange, and small red berries shine through the glass of these containers to become an integral part of the display.
above center Sea shells add their luminescence to a simple arrangement of white roses.
top Red and yellow sand cleverly layered in a glass flute are the perfect complement to a stunning primula.
above Black-and-white sand in a goblet-shaped glass vase gives a zebra-like effect that makes an effectively graphic contrast with the delicate lily of the valley.

left and right This softly romantic arrangement would make a beautiful table center for a wedding party. It stands in a plastic bowl covered with sprigs of broom, and tied with twine. The flowers I have used are ivory roses and creamy yellow freesias.

below Sprigs of Australian brush grass set the tone for a more regimented arrangement. Here the florist's foam does not come above the edge of the container, giving the brush grass and roses a squared-off, geometric look.

wealth of inspiration. One of my favorites is the broad ribbon with holes that is the result of punching sequins out of gold or silver foil. This gives a very lavish, festive appearance to any arrangement. Whatever you choose, a container you have made yourself will be unique.

To get you started, all you need is a plastic container and some double-sided tape or glue in a glue gun. Then simply stick your chosen material to the container. If you are using sprigs of foliage or leaves, it is sometimes useful to hold them in place with a large rubber band as you work. Once you have completely covered the plastic, finish off the container with a decorative tie of raffia, seagrass, or cord, then cut through the rubber band to remove it.

Thick twigs or small branches also make very beautiful one-off containers. Choose some that are of similar thickness and length—or cut them to length—and arrange them in pairs, each pair

one-off containers

To my mind, nothing beats making your own container. They are not difficult. I love them for a special event or to suit a particular interior.

If you use plant material to cover your container, it can look as if it is actually still growing. I love using sprigs of broom or rosemary, or large flat leaves like laurel, magnolia, or eucalyptus. You could also use cut lengths of bamboo, or even any plant material with an elongated form such as green beans, cinnamon sticks, celery, rhubarb, or asparagus.

If you prefer, you can cover your container with one of the many colored ribbons that are on the market, or perhaps with a thick cord or twine. Notions and stationery counters provide a

left and above A mass of acid-yellow amaryllis makes an eye-catching table center between two boldly blue sofas. The amaryllis have been specially dyed. A few sprays of matching oncidium orchids from Singapore add a touch of softness. In this instance the container has simply been covered with harmonizing loose-weave ribbon. This treatment is all that a contemporary room setting requires.

opposite, above Ranunculi in mixed colors are my all-time favorite flowers. To provide a cool contrast with the hot ranunculi, I covered the container with flat round eucalyptus leaves attached with double-sided tape.

opposite, below left Here I gave a festive twist to a plastic bowl by covering it with a length of punched gold ribbon and then arranging a few gold-sprayed curly pancho reeds across the top. The lovely salmon-colored 'Lambarda' roses have been left long to make a tall, showy arrangement. The florist's foam has been disguised with a scattering of orange gravel to complete the effect.

opposite, below right Thick cotton rope attached to double-sided tape turns a plain plastic bowl into an unusual summery container for an outdoor party. I placed a few white phalaenopsis orchids in phials of water and concealed them in the white sand filling the bowl. The result is neat and compact.

sitting on the last and at right angles to it. They should form a square. Now bind the whole thing together with string or raffia, then line it with heavy plastic sheeting. When you have filled it with flowers or bulbs, conceal any gaps with pieces of moss.

To hold flowers in place in a plastic-bowl container, pack the bowl with soaked florist's foam. For an arrangement with a rounded look, make sure the foam comes above the top of the container. Then your plant material can trail gently over the edges. For a more geometric look, like the wedge-shaped arrangement of roses on page 70, you will need to keep the foam in line with the top of the container. For large flowers with thick stems like amaryllis or hyacinths, it is better to use 2-inch chicken wire instead of florist's foam for support. Firmly attach the chicken wire to the bowl with florist's tape before you start positioning the flowers; otherwise, the arrangement will topple over.

Large fruits and vegetables can also make unusual one-off containers. They do not last long, but can be very effective for a special occasion. Hollow out the fruit or vegetable to remove its flesh, then line it with plastic. Arrange your flowers inside using soaked florist's foam. Traditionally, pumpkins are treated this way at Halloween, but there are other possibilities too. You can try any members of the squash family, especially gourds, as well as coconuts, globe artichokes, and melons, or, for smaller arrangements, even zucchini and peppers.

73

far left, left and below A container as bold as this one, with its wonderful wavy stripes that follow the curve of the vase, needs strongly graphic flowers that can hold their own. Here, from left to right, I have used three stems of 'Orca' gerberas with black-sprayed contorted willow; silver brunia with red 'Bacarolla' roses; and two specimens of 'Acropolis' anthuriums with contorted willow, again sprayed black.

classic terra-cotta

Terra-cotta—literally "fired earth"—is as old as civilization, and pots made from it are a must for flower arrangers.

Whether for plants or for floral displays held in soaked florist's foam, it makes the perfect container because it is porous and allows plants to breathe, yet retains water. It is also very inexpensive. You could easily make a number of arrangements in terra-cotta pots to give to your guests to take home after a party.

The classic terra-cotta pot shape is elegant and looks good just as it is, or with a bow or tie of raffia. Alternatively, you can transform it into something more glamorous with a few tricks. The simplest and most economical is to give it a lick of spray paint, or treat it to a special paint finish such as a crackle or verdigris finish. Another possibility is to mount the pot on an old record turntable and paint it in bands of color as it revolves, like making a pot on a potter's wheel. Or you may prefer to cover it with glued-on skeletonized leaves that reveal the terra-cotta beneath, or with mosaic for a contemporary look. Like a chameleon, a plain terra-cotta pot can adapt to almost any situation.

far left, clockwise A mixture of grape hyacinths, violets, anemones, and hydrangea heads tone with the blue-painted bands of their terra-cotta pot; deep pink late-flowering double tulips are loosely arranged in a terra-cotta pot decorated with a mosaic of glass; a handful of 'Mona Lisa Blue' anemones have been fashioned into a living topiary trimmed with moss and finished with a purple raffia tie; a gold-sprayed pot decorated with gold-sprayed skeletonized leaves holds a cluster of 'Black Beauty' roses encircling a chunky gold candle.
left A simple yellow ranunculus makes an eyecatching statement planted in a terra-cotta pot painted in harmonizing bands of color.

lavish wraps

If you get tired of using the same old glass vase over and over again, do not despair. Help is at hand. All you need to do is transform it with a wrapping of fabric to complement your flowers, held in place with double-sided tape, and lo and behold, you have a completely new look. Use the same trick to disguise any inexpensive vase. The only requirement is that it be shaped so that you can add on a tie and, unless you are working with opaque fabric, you should stick to using glass. The effect of stems seen through translucent fabric is very special.

With a bit of practice you will quickly get an eye for which fabrics look good with which flowers. Try taking a look around your local dress fabric store for gauzy chiffons, sinuous jerseys, and knobbly tweeds. And don't ignore the possibilities of furnishing fabrics. Net and muslin intended for drapes make some of the most dreamy, inexpensive wrappings you could hope to buy. Brocades will add a touch of stately-home grandeur, and linens are great for a rustic, homespun feel.

For country flowers like these narcissi, a wrap of burlap or linen is the perfect accompaniment, while for the more sophisticated look of the arum lilies, crushed velvet tied with a golden cord cannot be bettered. Whatever fabric you use, you can be sure it will set the tone for the whole arrangement.

left Burlap sacking tied with string suits the natural naïveté of these brave and bright spring-flowering 'Tahiti' narcissi with their twigs of hazel just coming into bud.
right Arum lilies, popularized by the Art Nouveau movement at the end of the nineteenth century, have a timeless sophistication. Here they look elegant in a vase lavishly wrapped in rich purple crushed velvet, a fabric that is reminiscent of that same era. The contrast between the yellow of the arum lilies and the purple velvet adds to the arrangement's feeling of richness and decadence.

above Gold-sprayed arum lilies, seductively translucent gold-speckled tulle, and gold ribbon blend together to produce a truly glitzy arrangement—just right for any glamorous party.

above right Red, silver, purple, and candlelight collaborate in the name of romance. Here I have used red skimmia, dark pink roses, and purple anemones arranged in a block of soaked florist's foam that also keeps the candle in place. The perfect arrangement for a candle-lit meal for two.

above right Lime green and pink produce a fun mélange. Great for a summer lunch party, this arrangement of ranunculi in shades of pink makes a daring contrast with its pink raffia-tied wrapping.

right Move away from traditional holiday decorations with this frosted shimmery mixture of spray-painted twigs, lotus flower seed heads, and natural spruce. A glittery silver fabric tied with silver cord, and a chunky silver candle add the finishing touch.

Fabric-wrapped vases can come come in many guises and many different sizes. If you want to make a large arrangement, try wrapping a plastic pot from a garden center with swathes of fabric to harmonize with the flowers, then tie it with furnishing or curtain trimming, or with heavy rope. Wrapping containers in fabric doesn't mean that you have to go overboard with frills and femininity. Strong colors and rich textures are very suitable for arrangements in male environments. For these situations, you could try bowls covered with suede-effect fabric, and tied with leather shoe laces.

right The most delicate tulle has been flamboyantly ruched around a glass vase to produce a wonderful fairytale-style display. The daintiness of the tulle echoes that of the sweet peas. The whole arrangement makes me think of a summer wedding on the lawn.

variations on a theme

Just as a simple vase may be transformed by fabric wraps to suit many different occasions, so a plain, straight-sided kitchen tumbler can be given a similar treatment. Simply think of it as an actor in a play who puts on a new costume and makeup for every part. You will be surprised at how versatile an ordinary tumbler can be.

Use a tumbler to make a miniature topiary tree. For this you will need to support the flowers in soaked florist's foam, concealing the foam with leaves, stems, or twigs glued to the outside. For a less formal alternative, arrange the flowers loosely and conceal the glass with a covering that complements the character of the flowers.

Alternatively, instead of concealing the glass, use it to flaunt the contents. Fill it with attractive material—tiny vegetables like cherry tomatoes or these vivid patty pan squash, a few pebbles, or some reeds, flexible young twigs, or small glossy leaves arranged so they twine around and conceal the flower stems.

left Soak a piece of florist's foam in water, then cut it to fit your tumbler. Stick dark magnolia leaves to the sides of the tumbler using a strong adhesive and tie a matching cord around the center. Arrange some mini sunflowers so their heads form a ball shape, then tie them just below the heads. Press the stems firmly into the foam for a topiary effect.

above Drop a few brightly colored patty-pan squash into the tumbler and fill it with water. Cut some stems of roses to size and arrange them among the patty pans so their heads just peep over the top edge of the tumbler.

right Take some heavy sisal twine and wrap it tightly around the tumbler, securing it at both ends with strong adhesive. Top up the tumbler with water and fill with an arrangement of safflowers, atriplex, hypericum, dill, and reed.

wrapped & tied

Receiving a gift of flowers is always a charming and uplifting experience. In our fast-moving, highly technological world, nothing is more blissful than a moment's pause to consider nature's work.

And when the flowers are beautifully presented, the experience is enhanced. Who would not be touched by the knowledge that someone has taken the trouble to select the perfect tie, the perfect paper, or the perfect leaf to wrap their gift?

In some cultures, such as the French and the Japanese, wrapping presents is an art form, and we can learn much from them. A gift of flowers is always to be treasured, but it can be enhanced by careful wrapping and presentation.

When I discovered the possibility of wrapping bouquets in natural leaves, it started me on a journey of experimentation. I began with glossy laurel and magnolia leaves, then moved on to tropical leaves. A foray to London's fruit and vegetable market, which is next door to the flower market, brought the discovery of the "filleted" banana leaf. At the flower market, banana leaves are sold with their inflexible central vein intact, but those that are on sale in the fruit market, shipped from Thailand for use in Asian cuisine, have the vein removed. This makes it easy to pleat the leaves around a bouquet .

But you do not have to resort to very unusual leaves to wrap a bouquet. The main requirements are that those you choose be medium to large in size and reasonably tough. Bear in mind, too, their color, and make sure it complements rather than overwhelms the flowers you are wrapping.

below Sea holly, celosia, and mixed tropical leaves make a very textural wrapped bouquet.
below center and below right A perfect gift is simply made by wrapping a single stem of hydrangea with aspidistra leaves, and tying it all with beargrass.

simple flowers

Once you start looking for leaves to use in this way, your eyes will be opened, as mine were, to the vast range of possibilities.

The large, glossy green perforated leaves of the Swiss-cheese plant, the long, lance-shaped leaves of the red cordyline, the broad plain and variegated leaves of the aspidistra, the wonderfully marked leaves of the calathea family, and the colorful leaves of the ornamental cabbage are probably available both at the market or in your own home or backyard. One or two of these will convert a few flower stems into a fascinating statement.

Using leaves to wrap gift flowers is not the only possibility, though. I am always on the search for new ideas. Among my favorite wrappings are beautiful textural handmade papers and translucent rice paper from the East. Crepe papers and tissue papers in all the colors of the rainbow are easy to find, and can be chosen to complement your flowers. At present, I am very fond of using translucent drawing paper printed with colored dots. Dotted paper is a classic. It always looks fun.

Sometimes all that is needed to make a bouquet out of the ordinary is a simple bow. Instead of the usual satin ribbon, try experimenting with textural ties like heavy grosgrain, cord, or natural or colored raffia or sisal.

There are also occasions when you can tie a bouquet with living material. Vines of honeysuckle make a heavenly fragranced tie for a late-spring or early-summer bouquet, while trails of scented jasmine or stephanotis are perfect for wedding bouquets.

near right A bunch of mixed stocks has been wrapped using hand-made gift wrap.
right, above An unusual bouquet combines carnations in jewel colors interwoven with ornamental cabbage leaves. The bouquet is tied with a broad, coarsely woven burlap ribbon in a toning color.
right, below I particularly like to see banana leaves wrapped around bouquets. Here they provide a a smart, snug jacket for a bunch of 'Ecstasy' roses. This rose has an aroma so delicious you could almost eat it.

this page 'Colombe de la Paix' arum lilies and stephanotis make an irresistible combination for a bridal bouquet. The stephanotis with its trailing stems of flowers and its waxy, silky leaves is exquisitely beautiful and fills the air with its heady scent.

When making a hand-tied bouquet like this one, it is important not to hold the stems too tightly or they will become warm and start to wilt. As you arrange the flowers, twist the stems slightly so they form a spiral. Remove any foliage from the stems beneath the binding point or "waist" of the bouquet.

Rather than a conventional floral centerpiece on a table, have some fun decorating each individual place setting. These work for anything from an informal dinner to a wedding party. You could try spraying a piece of fruit with silver or gold paint and putting one at each place. Spray lightly for a translucent effect, or several times for a more gilded appearance. Use a small trail of ivy to tie a crisp white napkin, or a few sprigs of lavender tied with a little raffia for the place settings at a summer dinner party. Glossy leaves, such as galax, laurel and rhododendron, make marvelous placecards. Wash or wipe the leaf and then let it dry before using a silver or a gold marker to write a name on the shiny side. Use the same idea to make a modest gift a little special, substituting a leaf for a gift tag. You could attach a gift-tag leaf to a tiny photograph album, box of pot-pourri or bag of chocolate almonds, and put one at each place for your guests to take home with them.

opposite page, left, from top to bottom A simple strand of ivy makes a napkin rather special; yellow Singapore orchids tied on with beargrass add a flavor of the Orient to a place setting; a gold cord and sprig of lavender lightly powdered with gold spray secure a napkin, while a gold-sprayed pear adds the finishing touch.
oppposite page, right Mark a place setting with three miniature anthuriums wrapped in a *Calathea insignis* leaf held in place with a tiny piece of raffia.
this page Add a touch of love with a glycerined magnolia leaf fashioned into a heart shape and secured to a guest napkin with raffia.

this page, clockwise A contemporary look is created with a few stems of snakegrass tied around a vase containing celosia and *Gloriosa superba*; arum lilies tied into a dumb-bell shape with stems of elephant grass make an unusual, easily held wedding bouquet; the yellow veins of the croton leaves covering a tall straight-sided glass and tied with golden cord echo the 'Golden Gate' roses.

opposite page, top row I love *Gloriosa superba* for their color and shape. When they are plentiful and relatively inexpensive, I like to use them *en masse*. Here they look elegant in a tall vase covered with aspidistra leaves.

opposite page, below A simple galvanized pot is given a new twist with some gold-sprayed pancho reeds twisted around it. The reeds are practical as well as decorative since they provide support for the delicately shaded cream and cerise-pink 'Laminuette' roses.

You can also transform a container into a living sculpture by wrapping it in leaves. All you need is some double-sided tape or carpet tape. Fix lengths of the tape around the container, then press your chosen leaves onto the tape's sticky surface. Alternatively, you can hold the leaf wrapping in place with a piece of cord or string, or with a plant material tie such as a length of beargrass or horsetail. Select the leaf to suit the size of container. Clearly a large banana leaf would swamp a small jelly jar, but three or four ivy leaves tied with raffia will quickly turn one into a container with a difference. You would never be able to tell how it started life!

The same rule applies to choosing leaves to wrap around a container as to choosing them to wrap a bouquet—they must be reasonably tough. There are many to choose from. Aspidistra leaves make an elegant choice for tall vases. If the vase has a foot, like the one shown here, the leaves can be made to fan out over it. Elaeagnus leaves are a good choice for creating silvery gray or variegated containers, while deep green galax leaves are attractive for their lovely, rounded heart shape. For everyday arrangements, the most inexpensive foliages to use are rhododendron or laurel. You can also cover a container with reeds or twigs using a glue gun on a low temperature to do so. If you add a few stems of cinnamon, you will have a fabulous container for a winter arrangement.

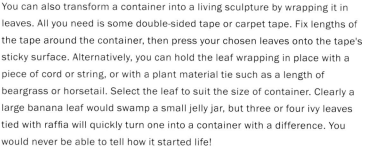

left and top Silver cord holds the heather in place around an arrangement of roses, orchids, and hebe. The flowers are in concentric circles, underlining the circular shape of the "cake" arrangement.

above Small bundles of paint-sprayed twigs held in place with raffia make a colorful edging to an arrangement of roses, arum lilies, and mixed foliage.

right A whole ornamental cabbage standing in the center of a mass of heather is simplicity itself.

far right Bundles of lavender tied to a twig basket make a deep edging for a mass of 'Extase' roses.

For something just that bit special on a birthday, why not try making a "flower cake?" They are time-consuming, but are always well received. When making one, bear in mind that the sides of the "cake" are just as important as its center, so spend some time considering what will give the best effect. For the sides, I like to use heathers, hebes, and protea foliage, as well as bundles of twigs, broom, or lavender.

Start with a deep basket. The depth is necessary since it is the sides of the "cake" that are most on show once it is on the table. Personally, I prefer to use a basket made of a mixture of twigs and chicken wire, but failing that, any basket will do as long as it has a loose weave.

Cut your edging material into pieces of uniform length and wire them into the basket. If you want bundles covering the sides, make the bundles first, tying them with pieces of string, raffia, or colored cord before wiring or tying each one in place. To finish, position the flowers for the center either in soaked florist's foam or in chicken wire held in place with florist's tape.

97

spring

Spring creeps up on us gently, calmly, and subtly. With its pure colors, clean shapes, and delicate fragrances, it is nature at its most beguiling and entrancing.

Slowly we become accustomed once more to the sight and scent of flowers in our gardens and homes. Coax the gentleness of spring into your arrangements by keeping them fresh and simple, allowing the onlooker to revel in the charming detail and quiet understatement of this contemplative time of year.

After the dark, evergreen foliage of barren winter has tended to dictate rich color schemes for flower arrangements, I feel that it is particularly appropriate for white or pastel flowers to hold sway in spring. White is also symbolic of the dawning of the new year. I am drawn to its purity as a reaction against the decorative excesses of the holiday season.

Curiously enough, although white flowers can be found throughout the world, they predominate in the colder northern climates. The bravest white flower, because it is the first to bloom after the festive season, is the delicate snowdrop. Its fragile appearance belies an exceptional hardiness: its fresh

green leaves and dainty, nodding flowers pierce the frozen ground and resist even the severest frosts to become the first harbinger of spring.

Pastel-pink tulips and hyacinths are other spring favorites of mine and are the most popular combination for posies on Mother's Day. Pale blue grape hyacinths and lily of the valley are often the choice of spring brides, and look beautiful woven into headdresses for blue-eyed flower girls. Peach-colored flowers are also enjoying a revival and there are now plenty to choose from in spring—heavenly scented peach hyacinths, fantastic peach and green Parrot tulips, long-stemmed French tulips, and dramatic amaryllis.

Yellow is another common color for spring flowers. It brings a touch of cheer after a long winter. In fact some anthropologists believe that the brain

far left Contorted willow combines with a planted cymbidium orchid for a fresh spring arrangement.
left Fill a flute vase with elephant grass and French tulips and watch the tulips move, craning their necks to steal as much light as possible.
right and below In this elegant arrangement, lengths of ivy are first wired around the rim of a metal basket-weave urn, then the body of the urn is packed with sheets of banana leaves. Finally, a glass cylinder is slipped inside the banana leaves and crammed with stems of flowering cherry.

confuses the luminous quality of yellow with sunlight, which increases our sense of well-being. Yellow is the color of cowslips, of some of the wallflowers, and of the daffodil, that most popular of spring flowers. It is also the color of many of the spring-flowering shrubs such as forsythia and mahonia.

My preferred spring flowers—in fact, I can never resist taking them home with me from my shop—are ranunculi. They have the most dainty tissuelike petals. Related to the common buttercup, they come in a beautiful range of colors and look charming simply arranged together. With their delicate texture and soft, rounded shape, they also suit inclusion in traditional mixed arrangements. They last for a long time too, and even as they fade and wither, are still good to look at.

The tulip is another favorite spring flower of mine. The Netherlands are justly famous for the mass of tulips that grow in the bulb fields in spring. A staggering four hundred different varieties are sold as cut flowers through the Dutch auctions at this time of year, and nothing provides a taste of spring quite like them. However, modern technology enables growers to "force" bulbs into flower early, by tricking them into thinking that the weather is getting warmer after the cold weeks of winter. So we can now enjoy them all year round.

According to the Dutch, who produce over 750 million tulips a year and who supply most of the demand across the world, yellow is top of the popularity stakes. In early and mid-spring I, for one, love the delicately scented sulfur-yellow

above Flowers can look lovely sandwiched between two glass dishes for a dinner-table arrangement. Carefully place the flowers on one dish and gently place another on top. Use the flower bowl to serve food or even fill it with water and float a few more blooms inside.
far left and left Brighten up the last few days of winter by packing a vase or container with flowers. Masses of California lilac and blue irises, or a clump of modest grape hyacinths, are sheer indulgence!
right Just a few beautiful freesias make us think of the scents and colors that the next few months have in store.

'Monte Carlo' and the lacy-edged buttercup-yellow 'Fringed Elegance.' I am also fond of the slightly later-flowering elegant long-stemmed French tulips. Most tulips do not have a scent, but 'Monte Carlo' and the sturdy orange 'Ad Rem' are among the few exceptions.

Unlike tulips, a number of spring flowers are renowned for their fragrance. Among these are the 'Paperwhite' narcissi. This faithful bulb is used by the Chinese to celebrate their new year. Whether cut or growing, narcissi are among the best room fragrancers I know. Violets also reach the flower markets at this time of year and are famous for their scent. I love the short-stemmed English violets as well as the world-renowned long-stemmed Parma violets. These are flown out from Italy tied in bunches with their lovely deep green leaves. Unfortunately, their vase life is very short. Perhaps that is what helps to make them so special.

For something a bit different, you could try edible flowers to accompany your table settings. In spring, pansies and violas are available. Their strong, bright faces make an interesting decoration when pressed between two glass platters, or you can simply scatter them on top of a salad.

Usually known in the kitchen for its seeds and bulb, the flowers of the fennel plant can also be eaten. When summer comes, the choice of edible flowers becomes even wider and includes nasturtiums, marigolds, borage and chive flowers, cornflowers and, of course, rose petals. If you are arranging flowers to eat, you should make sure they have been grown organically. Store-bought flowers have usually been specially treated to make them last longer, so the flowers you pick from the yard are best.

The striking red, orange, and yellow crown imperials, with their crownlike tuft of bright green leaves on their flowerheads, are among spring's most statuesque plants. If you want to grow them in your yard, you should plant them in the fall to flower the following spring. The reason so many of us adore these flowers is that they have a very limited season, so they are something of a prized possession. They have been popular with gardeners since the nineteenth century, but have only been cultivated commercially for the last few years. Some people do not like their pungent, garlicky smell, but I think that is a small price to pay for such a bold flower, which rearranges itself into ever more attractive shapes as it moves toward the light. Unusually, crown imperials also look wonderful when viewed from underneath, when you can see their lovely "teardrops." When you brush against them, they perform the magical feat of "crying." The teardrops are actually drops of nectar. Folklore has a touching tale that explains this phenomenon: when Christ was taken from the garden of Gethsemane to His crucifixion, the crown imperials were so sad that they bowed their heads in remorse and their petals filled with tears.

Originally from the Cape of Good Hope, the freesia is one of the most popular scented flowers in the world. They are certainly among the most requested blooms in my shop. They can now be bought at any time of the year, but they are really spring flowers. Their vase life is relatively short, so it is important to buy them at just the right stage of development—with one flower open and showing good color. They should last about a week and if you remove the flowers as they fade, that will encourage the unopened buds to bloom. I love their funnel-shaped flowers, especially in creamy-white, and often have a few on my dresser table in a simple container. Viewed singly, in twos or threes, or *en masse*, their unopened green buds add to their interesting shape. They are a popular choice for spring weddings.

above The sinuous flowing lines of sweet gale contrast with a cluster of straight, thick-stemmed 'Aladdin' tulips. The red frosted glass vase is the perfect partner for the color of the tulips.
right 'Rapid Red' freesias make a boldly colored spring arrangement. Cut all the freesias to the same length and insert them in soaked florist's foam in a galvanized pot, finishing the design off with with red-sprayed gravel.
opposite Crown imperials look majestic in a classical glass urn on a tall pedestal. The detail shows the crown imperial's beautiful "teardrops" inside each flower.

far left, above and center left The combination of pinks and greens is always fresh-looking. Here anemones, guelder roses, lilac, gaultheria, and limes have been arranged in florist's foam so they tumble gently over the rim of a galvanized vase. If you want to use fruit in an arrangement, as here, you should mount each piece on thick wire to help position it.

far left, below Line an urn-shaped basket with heavy plastic sheeting, fill it with soaked florist's foam, and make a simple spring display of mixed red, pink, and purple 'Mona Lisa' anemones.

above Hot-colored ranunculi—my favorite spring flowers—look theatrical planted in small glass tanks lined with gravel in contrasting shades.

summer

Summer brings in its train a cornucopia of riches for the flower arranger. But the sheer abundance of flowers and foliage can be a mixed blessing.

If you are confused about where to begin, do not despair. Think simple. Stick to a limited color palette and a few choice specimens. Often a handful of carefully chosen flowers combined with a striking leaf or two will make the biggest impact of all.

tall & stately

This understated green and white composition is made up of just two elements—aspidistra leaves and chincherinchees. Apsidistra makes a natural wrapping and, as the name by which it sometimes known—the cast-iron plant—suggests, is very robust. The starry Arabian chincherinchee is a long-lasting flower for hot, sunny days. Its tall stems make it very architectural. It is also very versatile. It survives well in florist's foam and its tiny flowerets can be wired into a headdress for a bride or flower girl. Available all year round, it can last up to three weeks in the correct conditions. If you wish, you could cut the stems of this arrangement down to make an attractive gift bouquet.

Cut the chinchirinchees to length. **Starting** at the center, arrange in concentric circles. **Make** a domed effect with the flowers slightly higher at the center. **Tie** them just below the "waist" with raffia. **Bend** each aspidistra leaf and use to edge the chincherinchees. **Tie** the arrangement with another piece of raffia, leaving the ends loose. **Trim** the aspidistra stems at an angle. **Stand** the arrangement in the vase.

Flowers:
20 stems Arabian chincherinchee
2 bunches aspidistra leaves

As spring unfolds into summer, many of the jewels of my native England's floral landscape herald the beginning of warmer weather. The country's natural woodlands, covered with spectacular carpets of color as the bluebells push their way up under the trees, are truly inspiring.

Early summer is one of my favorite times of year. In England, these weeks lead up to the world-famous Chelsea Flower Show, marking the beginning of the summer season. It is also a time when some of my favorite British flowers—delphiniums, peonies, and the wonderful, arched stems of Solomon's seal—appear in all their finery. As summer progresses, gardens become a riot of color. Flower shops and stalls overflow with the staples of summer—lavender, snapdragons, marigolds, roses, sweet peas, stocks,

tobacco plants, lilies, and phlox. I particularly love the flower arrangers' acid-green summer favorites—bells of Ireland and lady's mantle.

In midsummer the color blue comes into its own. Many blue flowers are particularly attractive because of their form and scale. I love the wiggly spires of veronica and the whiskers of love-in-the-mist, and who can resist the blue of the wonderful dainty bachelor's button that grows among the ripening wheat in the fields? Spiky sea holly and boldly elegant agapanthus are other blue flowers of the summer that I find delectable whatever the interior.

Late summer is a mellow, yellow period for me. This is a time for using sunflowers and *Achillea* 'Gold Plate' together with evening primroses. It is also the best time for the cottage-garden scabious. Helenium and rudbeckia combine well in arrangements with stems of foxtail lily, red-hot poker, and the climber sandersonia. Foxtail lilies, especially, last well, even in the heat of summer. Sandersonia is a recent addition to European floristry. Its delicate little bells resemble the flowers of the orange Chinese lantern, but it has arched, slightly drooping stems. I find that it is easily overpowered by other flowers, so is best admired on its own.

In summertime, the traditional choice is for large massed arrangements that look as if they have just been picked from the garden—armfuls of buddleja, night-scented stocks, richly textured larkspur, dainty clematis, and perhaps also some of the rich offerings of the edible garden—herbs, salad leaves, globe artichokes.

opposite, left A few stems of sandersonia arranged in a Venetian-style glass vase look bright in late summer.
opposite, right For a bold, minimal statement, all you need is a couple of red-hot pokers in a sinuous narrow-necked white-glazed vase.
left A frosted yellow vase echoes the color of some stately foxtail lilies. Tall flowers like these require a tall vase.

113

right and below This arrangement with its linear lines betrays its oriental influence. It consists of green bells of Ireland, green *Dendranthemum* 'Shamrock,' blue agapanthus, creamy 'Colombe de la Paix' arum lilies, a single 'Midori' anthurium, and a stem of contorted willow. 'Midori' is Japanese for "green." This beautiful green anthurium is very popular because its color helps many combinations along.

opposite Three paphiopedilum orchids go on stark display in a coordinating green-glazed vase. This orchid is a favorite with photographers, who love the insectlike appearance of this long-lasting but short-stemmed bloom. Orchids are now available all year round, but are best in summer since they do not like temperatures below about 45 degrees. All orchids are also sensitive to the ethylene gas that is given off when plants age, so it is best to arrange them on their own and give them some flower food, which acts as an antibacterial agent. In these conditions, orchids can last many weeks.

But summer is a tricky time for novice flower arrangers who can be so overwhelmed with choice that they cram as much as possible into a vase and lose their sense of what looks good together and in what proportions. For them, especially, the best approach is to concentrate on just one or two choice varieties. Then the flowers will have a chance to speak for themselves. This minimal look is slowly supplanting massed, mixed arrangements and is more in tune with today's crisp, clean interiors.

The move toward a highly sculptural look has been helped along by the widespread importing of beautiful tropical flowers and foliage. These are so stunning that they often look best on their own, or with just one or two other choice specimens. Graphic, sculptural anthuriums and orchids, which withstand warmer temperatures, make excellent cut flowers and are a good choice for really hot days.

Tropical leaves and foliage provide sturdy foils for summer flower arrangements. They are now imported from all over the world, particularly from Africa, India, Sri Lanka, Israel, Australia, the West Indies, and South America. There is always a reluctance, though, on the part of customers to pay for foliage. They often think of it as an extra, but some stems and leaves can be more expensive than flowers.

If you are stuck and find it difficult to purchase interesting leaves and plant material, you could consider cutting up a house plant. The graphic leaves of the Swiss-cheese plant, the textural and colorful leaves of the *Begonia rex*, and the long, sword-like leaves of mother-in law's tongue are just a few of the common house plant leaves that would serve the purpose. Many of us harbor a weak specimen at home. In the interests of new, creative flower arrangements, now is the time to sacrifice it.

Gerberas and arum lilies are two of the flower arranger's favorites. The gerbera is so popular that over five hundred colors pass through the Dutch auctions every year, and some growers produce as many as two hundred. The success or failure of any particular one depends as much on its longevity as on its color. The exotic shape and beautiful bright hues of arum lilies have guaranteed them a place in the hearts of floral designers and style *aficionados*. They are surprisingly tough, thinking nothing of being swathed in foam and flown halfway across the world.

late summer's orange

Mangoes The brightly colored 'Mango' arum lily used here was once a rarity that I had to buy in New Zealand. Now, fortunately, it is easier to obtain, and I have made full use of the stunning impact of its color by placing a mass of them in a simple glass vase. First, I filled the vase with florist's foam, then cut lengths of snakegrass to fit around the edges and conceal the foam from view. I then positioned the arum lilies to make a slightly domed shape and finished the arrangement off with a collar of shiny, heart-shaped galax leaves that serve to hide any gaps.

Orange suns The miniature gerberas used here were specially cultivated to answer the need for a gerbera that could be used in small hand-tied posies. They are known as "germini." As you can see, they are also very effective on their own and make a simple, economical display. Whichever gerberas you buy, be sure they are in good condition, with stiff stems and undamaged petals. If you look closely at their stems, you will see that they are very hairy. This indicates that they do not like to stand in deep water. Correctly treated, they can last up to three weeks, and growers are continually devising ways of producing varieties that last even longer. This arrangement consists of nothing more than a few stems of germini in an interesting sectioned aluminum vase. The vase is given a lift with some bright-colored florist's wire to blend with the flowers. The gray-orange contrast is stunning!

It is not until harvest time in late summer that I think about orange as a summer color, but then I really go to town with it. French marigolds and nasturtiums rapidly become part of my floral palette, and I love to mix red-hot pokers with blue globe thistles, or orange gladioli with tall spires of bells of Ireland or with dark burgundy gladioli. Other orange favorites of mine for late summer are dahlias, crocosmia, safflowers, *Celosia* 'Persimmon Chief,' *Antirrhinum* 'Potomac Orange,' *Alstroemeria* 'Little Sun,' Chinese lanterns, *Hypericum* 'Pink Flair,' blood flowers, and some of the foxtail lilies. They all work well with the dark burgundy foliage of leucadendron, *Photinia* 'Red Robin,' and the all-time favorite, the smoke bush. There are also some wonderful, long-lasting Asiatic lilies in shades of orange—'Beatrix,' 'Avignon,' and 'Monte Negro' are three examples that all mix well with pincushion flowers and with mauve and purple flowers such as gayfeathers, lisianthus, and trachelium. The arrival of berries on the scene gives me even more flower-arranging possibilities—there are the rich orange-red berries of the guelder rose, and the pinkish-orange berries of the pistachio to play around with. But my all-time favorite summer orange is the zinnia, long popular in the United States and just beginning to catch on elsewhere. They appear in stunning shades of orange, and I love the way their petals have a ruffled, antique-looking edge.

autumn

As summer merges gently into fall, the color brown begins to dominate the landscape around us. But nature simply does not know how to be uniformly, boringly brown.

Instead, she clothes herself in a dazzle of colors from russet through red and orange to chestnut. Golden yellow fields are shorn, then turn chocolate brown. Trees become fiery red, then reveal their barren branches. These are the rich, opulent shades that set the pace indoors as well as out.

At this time of year, I tend, almost unconsciously, to use the brown palette of colors. True brown flowers are rare, but many within this range have become fashionable in recent years. The brownish-red 'Leonidas' rose and the mango-colored arum lily are two examples. One of the most stylish flowers I have ever seen is the dark, velvety chocolate cosmos, while the appropriately named 'Choco' anthurium is one of the strangest of the brown flowers.

Brown is also frequently present in the centers of flowers, and in the fall I enjoy using flowers without their petals in order to emphasize this feature. Sunflowers look shaggy when their petals are damaged, but if you gently pull them all off, the brown centers can add interesting texture to an arrangement. I even glue the centers around pots to make fascinating autumn-flower containers. However, for me, rudbeckia is top of the league of flowers to use in this unusual way.

Brown is of course also present in stems, branches, and berries. I love the contorted willow that comes on the market when its leaves have fallen. It is

something of a luxury item, but can be used time and time again if disinfected with bleach between arrangements. My favorite brown, however, is that of the hypericum berry, which is brilliant as a filler and also adds texture. Originally appearing only in late summer and fall, it is now available every week of the year.

The fieriness of orange makes it a challenging color and one that really comes into its own each Halloween and Thanksgiving. As winter approaches, we are automatically drawn to cheery colors to warm and brighten up the days as they become shorter and colder.

left and above left Place a small glass tank inside a larger one and fill the space between with dyed Spanish moss. Pack marigolds into the smaller tank so their heads just peek over the top.
above The arching stems of a 'Cambria Plush' orchid in a rusted urn topped off with sphagnum moss look fetchingly elegant. This orchid is a splendid autumnal red.

autumnal roses

The rose was once the queen of the summer garden, but it now exists in hundreds of varieties all year round. When autumn arrives, there is no longer any need to wave goodbye to them in your arrangements. They can continue being used well into the fall and beyond. These beautiful arrangements were photographed when autumn was well underway.

Just twenty years ago, few roses were scented, but recent developments mean that now more than fifty scented ones are grown, and I see a new variety nearly every week at London's Covent Garden Market. Very fragrant cultivars include the dark pink 'Jacaranda' and the dark red 'Extase.'

Other developments include two-tone roses that give the flower arranger opportunities for new color combinations. There are the "edged" varieties, such as 'Confetti,' which is yellow edged with orange, and the popular bridal rose, 'Laminuette,' which is cream with a cerise-pink edge.

The most recent trendsetters, though, have been the "inside-out" varieties of roses. These roses have petals that are one color on the outside and another color on the inside. One of the curent best-sellers of this type has been the 'Leonidas' rose, with petals that are a uniquely beautiful brownish-red on the outside and red on the inside.

In the past, commercial growers found it difficult to produce roses that opened well. Often their heads drooped and remained obstinately closed. Things are different now. The orange 'Rising Sun' rose is one that gives great value for money. Its flowers are guaranteed to open into well-formed, rounded, sculptural shapes that give a great deal of pleasure. I love to use it with the multicolored leaves of the croton plant. Another modern development is the 'Gypsy Curiosa' rose. This opens beautifully just like

traditional garden roses, but lasts as well as commercially grown ones. First grown in Holland, the breeder has called it 'Curiosa' because of its unusual rusty-orange color. It looks stunning with other fall material.

In their search for the perfectly natural-looking rose, commercial growers have also developed the spray rose. More like garden roses than some of the other commercially grown varieties, spray roses are now very popular. For an autumnal orange, choose the red-and-yellow variegated 'Rumba,' the spray-rose version of the hot orange 'Lambarda.'

opposite, left and right This simple arrangement consists of nothing more than thirty-five 'Rising Sun' roses in a square terra-cotta pot, secured in florist's foam, and edged with croton leaves.

above, left and right You can make a dramatic autumnal arrangement by mixing a mass of 'Gypsy Curiosa' roses with beech leaves and pine cones. Other beautiful additions to roses in autumn are heathers, crab apples, the black berries of *Viburnum tinus*, rose hips, and crocosmia berries.

opposite Colorful votive candle-holders make quirky containers for miniature arrangements, especially at a time of year when the choice of material is becoming limited. Here I have filled a collection with cacti and arranged them around a larger pot holding vine leaves and hypericum berries.

center A splash of autumnal color is provided by an arrangement of mixed zinnias in a red-painted, plastic-lined plywood basket.

top Gerberas in mixed colors with an edging of bun moss contrast with an unusual galvanized container.

above Autumnal russets and yellows come together in an arrangement of 'Papillon' and 'Bacarolla' roses, *Bupleurum griffithii*, lilac, and greenish-yellow dill.

winter

Winter is rich in possibilities. Far from being the dullard in the flower arranger's calendar, it is a season of bold contrasts and dramatic statements.

Stark, ethereal displays of bare twigs and branches capture the spirit of the winter landscape. Jewellike colors and the hint of precious metals set the tone for festive occasions. Exotic blooms transport you to sun-filled, palm-fringed shores where winter's icy grip is unknown.

green & white

Green is a color that really comes into its own at holiday time when many people follow the age-old tradition of bringing evergreen plant material indoors. This tradition goes back to pagan times—the Roman festival of Saturnalia and the Yuletide celebrations of northern Europe. These took place around the winter solstice, when the days were at their shortest. They celebrated the new cycle of growth and fertility which the lengthening days would bring. Evergreens, revered because they symbolized the continuity of life, always played their part in the festivities, but because of this pagan association, it was thought to be unlucky to bring evergreens indoors. At Christmas time, however, there is enough goodwill around to ward off evil spirits.

Green and white look good in any surroundings and suit most tastes. There is something very soothing about it as a color combination. It's also a safe choice when you are starting out arranging flowers. Here I have used it to make a strongly textural winter wreath. To balance the textures, you need bold flowers like these anthuriums and amaryllis.

Immerse a florist's-foam wreath frame with a plastic base in water for five minutes. **Cut** sprigs from the foliage and use to cover the frame loosely. **Position** the papyrus heads evenly around the frame. **Add** three groups of amaryllis. To prevent their stems from splitting when you position them, first wrap the ends in cellophane tape. **Finally** add three clusters of anthuriums. Don't touch their spadices since damaging them will shorten the flowers' life.

Flowers:

1 or 2 branches *Berzelia galpinii*
1 branch *Viburnum grandiflorum*
6 heads papyrus
6 'White Dazzler' amaryllis
3 'Midori' anthuriums
3 'Acropolis' anthuriums

this page A mixed posy is possible even in the depths of winter. Here I have used white lilac, white 'Bianca' roses, ornamental cabbage, and *Skimmia japonica* 'Rubella.'
right, above An arrangement in russet shades consists of 'Leonidas' roses and autumnal oak leaves in a pot covered with cinnamon sticks secured with a seagrass tie.
right, below In a simple white vase filled with heads of papyrus, the reddish 'James Storey' orchids pick up the color of the spadices of the 'Acropolis' anthuriums.

Winter can be difficult for flower arrangers. In the northern hemisphere, the choice of seasonal flowers is severely limited, although thanks to modern horticultural advances, much plant material can now be obtained all year round. But I don't like arrangements that rely only on out-of-season material, completely ignoring the fact that it's winter. Instead, whenever I can, I like to incorporate some wintry element, whether in the form of seasonal foliage, twigs, or food from the winter kitchen, such as dried herbs or spices.

The latter conjure up the spirit of winter in an especially evocative way. Cinnamon has long been used in cooking and in perfumes. It is the dried bark of the *Cinammomum zeylanicum* tree, and is a long-standing favorite of mine, thanks to the wonderful spicy scent and rustic texture that it brings to winter arrangements. Dried bay leaves are something else to borrow from the winter kitchen. Glued around a container, they also add texture and aroma.

Among the many evergreens that are valuable for arrangements at this time of year, *Skimmia japonica* is one of my favorites. It not only has beautiful shiny, sharp-edged foliage that adds dramatic texture, but the dark red color of its unopened flowerets brings depth of tone to any design.

The ornamental cabbage also has great staying power through the long winter months, and it makes a superb filler. It is available in green and white—the white is almost a vanilla color—or dark purple shades that are splendid for making jewel-colored winter combinations gel.

Winter foliage comes into its own when you mix and match it. Try making a centerpiece for a long table using small ceramic pots, each filled with different foliage—*Brunia alopecuroides*, eucalyptus, hebe, *Garrya elliptica*, *Viburnum tinus,* and box are just a few of the foliages you can try.

Preserved autumnal foliages such as oak and beech leaves are another useful element at this time of year. Their rich browns and russets and striking texture blend well with other wintry materials. They are preserved by

top Individual flowers of dark red 'Liberty' amaryllis fill a terra-cotta pot painted with harmonizing red and cream stripes. The coils of fine gold-sprayed ting-ting reed from Thailand add the finishing touch.

above Pine cones have been sprayed bronze and glued onto sticks that act as stems. Casually arranged in a simple bronze vase, they make an unusual feature standing on a washbasin, where their color echoes that of the mirror frame above.

right The heads of tulips have a tendency to flop. To counteract this, these vanilla-colored French tulips have been tied with cord and stand erect in a matching pot above a collar of ornamental cabbages.

far right Beautiful specimens of 'Flaming Parrot' tulips give an unusual effect as they appear to cascade out of a glass vase filled with contorted willow.

soaking in a solution of glycerin and can last up to six months, so they are great value for money.

Moving on to out-of-season ingredients for winter arrangements, I like to use lots of silver and gray foliages. They have a wintry feel and, being lighter in tone than all other foliages and flowers except white, complement nearly every other color, providing an excellent foil for the bright and brash colors of the festive season. You can even combine them with painted, dipped, or sprayed foliages and seed heads—something that is very useful at this time of year.

Gray and silver foliages also often have interesting shapes and can be covered in a mass of tiny, fine hairs that make them glisten. In this respect they resemble Marilyn Monroe, whose skin was covered with fine blond hairs so that she positively glowed on screen. In the same way, silver foliage can become the star of your festive season.

Tropical imports provide another range of possibilities for winter. The highly textural spiky heads of papyrus look great on their own or, if you want to add some color, combined with other tropical material such as orchids and anthuriums. When you buy it, papyrus often looks disheveled, but it's simple to clean it up into a sharp, geometric shape with scissors.

In the northern hemisphere, it is around the holidays that the first spring flowers become available. My favorites are the elegant long-stemmed tulips raised in the South of France and sold in the flower market at Nice. Their bold shapes look spectacular on their own or combined with material that is equally graphic, such as contorted willow stems or the rounded heads of ornamental cabbages. A few of these tulips in your room will truly make you feel that spring is just around the corner.

For relief from the excesses of Christmas decorations, I often find the architectural quality of a simple arrangement of twigs refreshing. Twigs first come on the market in the fall when the sap has fallen and they can be gathered.

Contorted willow, with its sinuous, graphic lines, or the gnarled and lichen-covered stems from apple trees, will add interest to any winter arrangement. I also like the simple, bare stems of dogwood. These long, straight, strong-looking stems are available in the deepest red, green, or yellow. They make colorful arrangements that do not need any other adornment.

In addition to twigs, there is an increasing number of pods and seed heads grown especially for the flower-arranging trade. I like using lotus-flower and poppy-seed heads.

For "alternative" winter displays, I often turn to fruits and vegetables. I have recently become interested in the arts and crafts of the Native American tribes. If you travel through the American southwest after the pepper harvest, you will see many examples of wreaths and swags made entirely of dried chili peppers. Their graphic quality and muted shades of red, orange, and yellow will bring color into your home during the long months of winter.

opposite, left The gnarled stems of apple wood make a striking contrast with a cluster of velvety bulrushes.
opposite, right A mass of dogwood stems bursts out from an austere terra-cotta vase.
left This wreath of contorted willow has been fashioned without using any wire. When winter has passed, you can put it outside where the warm spring sunshine will make it sprout as if by magic.
below This bold dried chili-pepper wreath brings a touch of bright color to my own kitchen in winter.

left Make an arrangement with a Yuletide flavor from 'Nicole' roses, gold-sprayed ting-ting, and *Skimmia japonica* in a hollowed-out log.

top A Christmas classic consists of 'Leonidas' roses, hypericum berries, rudbeckia, *Skimmia japonica*, bupleurum, and gold ting-ting with a beeswax candle.

above 'Bacarolla' roses are tightly packed with gold-sprayed leaves in a gold star-shaped vase.

right Sprayed vines are used to make an unusual support for a festive display of spruce and holly.

far right Mini Yuletide trees stand in pots painted in bright oranges and yellows.

As Christmas approaches, the commercial flower markets are full of material that has been sprayed, dipped, or dyed. It is a time of year when it's easy to lose one's sense of taste in the pursuit of razzmatazz and glitz.

One of my favorite floral "extras" is the curly ting-ting reed. Grown in Thailand, it starts life straight but is curled while still green. I prefer it natural, but paint-sprayed, gilded, or covered with glitter, it is a maximum-impact item at Christmas.

Vines can also be sprayed, and have two important functions for the Christmas decorator. They may provide the basis for a garland, or they can be used in a vase to support foliages and flowers, producing a natural, very simple effect.

Mini Christmas trees are easy to construct and are lovely gifts for children to make and give. Cut a block of florist's foam to fit a pot, then shape the top of the foam into a cone. Cut foliage into short sprigs, trim the leaves off the base of the stems, then push them into the cone. You can tie toffees or candy to the foliage if you want.

This arrangement would grace any mantelpiece beautifully at Christmas. It consists of branches of holly and lichen-covered larch twigs carefully arranged with sprayed vines, red apples and grapes, and large obelisk-shaped candles. The candles are placed far enough away from the wall so they do not damage the paint.

care & maintenance

The most important factor for beautiful flower arrangements is the selection of good-quality plant material. It is also important to condition this material well.

If you are harvesting flowers from your own yard, take a bucket of water with you and place the stems in it immediately after cutting. Collect flowers in the morning before the sun gets too high and avoid plant material with new growth because this will often become limp and look unsightly.

If you are buying flowers, choose your retailer carefully. Have a look at the condition of the stock and don't be afraid to ask about the age of the flowers and their life expectancy. Most fresh flowers should last around five days, although delicate, fragile ones and scented varieties, such as sweet peas and stocks, may not be so longlasting. Most commercially grown flowers are treated after harvesting to improve their longevity, but owing to the additional labor involved, you must be prepared to pay a little extra.

A number of garden flowers and some of the very luxurious varieties do not last long at all, so are best saved for special events when it is more important for the flowers to look perfect for a day than to last a week.

Arranging flowers can be dirty and can damage furnishings and fabrics. To avoid any problems, always cover your work surface with heavy plastic or a large garbage bag. Choose your flowers carefully and look for tight buds and firm green stems and foliage. Once you get them home, recut the stems as soon as possible using a sharp knife and removing at least an inch. Make a diagonal cut to expose the maximum surface area to the water. Don't hammer the stems or split them, as this is now thought to prevent them taking up water. It is worth investing in a good pair of florist's scissors and a sharp garden knife.

Flowers with nodules along their stems, such as carnations, should be cut just above the nodule.

Before arranging the flowers, strip off all the leaves below the water level, or they will pollute the water.

Some material survives better if all the leaves are removed. Sunflowers and celosia are thirsty flowers that cope better when not competing for water with their foliage. Even the longlasting chrysanthemum will do better with most of its foliage removed.

Before arranging your flowers, condition them by giving them a good, deep drink. They absorb half the water they require to survive during the first twenty-four hours.

Narcissi exude slime from their stems which can damage other plant material in the same arrangement. To prevent this, condition them on their own for twenty-four hours. There are some flower foods on sale that are specially designed for use with narcissi in mixed arrangements.

Take care when handling flowers and foliage from the spurge family. They exude a latexlike substance that can cause irritation to the skin and eyes. It is best to wear latex gloves when handling this material, though I prefer to feel what I am working with. I simply take care to wash my hands and avoid touching my face or eyes. Normally any reaction is short lived, but should irritation persist, you should consult your doctor.

Many tropical leaves have a sticky residue on their surface when they are purchased. To remove this, wash with a plant mister or dunk in water, then leave to dry naturally before arranging.

Use tepid water to arrange your flowers because oxygen travels more easily through it and up into the stems. I always recommend adding flower food. It not only feeds the flowers and encourages buds to develop, but also prevents bacteria growing. Frequent changes of water are also very important if you want to keep your arrangements looking good for a long time.

Another essential rule is to keep your containers spotlessly clean and to wash them with a solution of bleach before storing them.

For the most beautiful results, support your cut flowers and foliage either with chicken wire, with a grid of household or florist's tape across the top of the container, or with a natural support such as twigs, foliage, or pebbles. Florist's tape is also invaluable for fixing chicken wire or foam in place.

Fine garden canes are essential for keeping the stems of planted amaryllis and orchids upright, and can also be inserted into the hollow stems of cut flowers such as delphiniums and lupines for

support. Amaryllis, for example, are so heavily hybridized that their heads are sometimes too heavy for their stems.

Flowers arranged in florist's foam will not last as well as in water, so foam should be saved for special occasions. Also, foam has a tendency to clog up stems, especially hollow stems such as those of amaryllis or hyacinths. In addition, hollow stems sometimes split when placed in foam. To prevent this, you should first wrap the ends in cellophane tape.

If you are using florist's foam, never dunk it in a bucket of water to soak it, but instead allow it to descend of its own accord. In this way it will absorb the water uniformly. And never attempt to reuse florist's foam as it fails to hold water a second time.

A cool room is better for prolonging the life of flowers, but note that if the room is too cool, scented flowers may not release their perfume fully. In general, you should avoid placing your displays in direct sunlight, heat, and drafts.

Some flowers, such as phalaenopisis orchids and violets, benefit from being submerged in water for up to an hour if they wilt. You can also intensify the color of anemones by dunking them in water before you arrange them.

Ethylene is a natural substance produced by flowers, plants, and fruit, but it also causes aging, so you should remove dead flower heads and leaves as they occur. For the same reason, unless you want to create a special effect, avoid placing cut flowers near fruit.

143

acknowledgments

When I began this project, I was unaware that, in 1935, the famous English floral artist Constance Spry, had published a book called *Simple Flowers*. While our perception of simplicity has changed over the last fifty years or so, many of the principles laid down by Constance are still relevant today. I would like to acknowledge my debt to her flower school for teaching me the rudiments of floristry and for starting me off on my new life with flowers.

Each day my inspiration comes from my early-morning visits to the New Covent Garden Market at Nine Elms in London. Over the ten years that I have been making these visits, I have formed many friendships and I am obliged to all the wholesalers there who have helped me. In particular, I am indebted to Dennis Edwards at John Austin for his constant support and dedication. Thanks also to Eric, Tom, and Matt.

I feel very privileged to have worked with the very talented James Merrell. The excellence of his photographs makes his hectic schedule understandable. James is deservedly respected and is an artist whose unstinting professionalism is an inspiration to us all.

My staff at the shop, my contract staff, delivery team, office staff, and freelance staff are all very talented and loyal. Thank you for all your hard work, for the long hours you put in, and for your dedication to the world of flowers.

I am particularly grateful to those who have worked directly on the production of this book: Ashleigh Hopkins; Joan Cardoza; Anita Everard; Sophie Hindley; Shinako Atsumi; Mikiko Tanabe; Hiroko Odakura; Yoko Okazaki; Fumiko Inoue; Atsuko Hata; and Noriko Kobayashi.

I also owe a huge debt to Jacqui Small for introducing me to the world of publishing and thereby making my style known throughout the world of flower arranging. I am grateful to her for suggesting this project to me and for setting the style of this book in such an inimitable way.

Penny Stock has been a calming influence during our hectic shoots and has to be congratulated for keeping me on target and for fitting all James Merrell's images into a manageable form. As I often take my inspiration from the flowers I find each day in the market, this had to be a book without a flat plan. That made Penny's task much more difficult.

In the pursuit of interesting interiors, fabulous vases, containers and props, Martin Bourne, with his assistant Emma, has trailed through all the best apartments in London and just about every shop in the capital. I am grateful to him for sharing his sense of style and good humor with us. Thanks to him also for arranging for us to photograph my flowers in such wonderful interiors, and thanks to everyone who allowed us into their homes.

Jane Struthers has woven her own brand of magic on the text and has, as always, been a long-suffering and loyal editor. It is my very special pleasure to work with her and to share her insights on life.

And a huge thank you to Hilary Mandleberg, who took over as my editor at the last minute, for her encouragement and understanding.

I would also like to thank Andrew Weaving of Century Design, London, for always thinking of me when he has something interesting in his wonderful shop, and also Richard Henham of The Chocolate Factory, London, for the fabulous pots on pages 32–3 and 50 (below). Thank you to Chris Johnson at Sia Parlane for advice, support, and insights, and thanks to the many friends I have made in Japan, and especially to Sawako Matsuoka who made the beautiful mosaic pot on page 76.

My family has been a constant support throughout my life, and I would like to say a special thank you to my parents who allowed me to hide out in their home while I was trying to finish the text. I really appreciate your love and advice, and thanks for all the pampering!

Finally, thank you to Peter Romaniuk, my husband, who over the years has come to terms with the fact that flowers are my whole life and who has had to share me with them. Peter has always preferred the simple beauty of flowers. It is he who has provided the inspiration for this book.